BUILDING UP ZION'S WALLS

Ministry for Empowering the African American Family

JAMES C. PERKINS

Edited by Jean Alicia Elster

Judson Press

Valley Forge

Building Up Zion's Walls:
Ministry for Empowering the African American Family

Unless otherwise indicated, Bible quotations in this volume are from *The Holy Bible,* King James Version.

Bible quotations designated NIV are from HOLY BIBLE: *New International Version,* copyright © 1973, 1978, 1984. Used by permission of Zondervan Bible Publishers.

Library of Congress Cataloging-in-Publication Data

Perkins, James C.
Building up Zion's walls : ministry for empowering the African American family / James C. Perkins ; edited by Jean Alicia Elster.
p. cm.
Includes bibliographical references.
ISBN 0-8170-1337-7 (pbk. : alk. paper)
1. Church work with Afro-American families. 2. Afro-American families – Religious life. I. Elster, Jean Alicia. II. Title.
BV4468.2.A34P47 1999
261.8′34896073 – dc21 99–27907

Printed in the U.S.A.

06 05 04 03

10 9 8 7 6 5 4 3

Contents

Foreword

Dr. Jawanza Kunjufu

For over twenty-three years I have spoken on solutions for the African American family at various conferences around the country. If, however, conferences could save us, we would not be wrestling with the same social dislocations as we approach the year 2000 that we have been wrestling with for the past twenty-five or even fifty years. The problem with most conferences is that no plans come out of them. There are rarely any follow-up initiatives.

That is not the case, however, with the 1997 National African American Family Ministry Conference and the book *Building Up Zion's Walls*, which is a direct result of those proceedings. The purpose of the conference was to introduce workable, useable models to those in attendance, which they, in turn, could *take back to their churches and communities* and use to build up and regenerate the African American families in their midst. This book is a continuation of that plan. Within its pages are examples from some of the most dynamic leaders and most effective ministries in the country of how to address the crisis issues affecting the African American family today. We'll take a look at several of the programs established by the author, the Reverend James C. Perkins, who is pastor of Greater Christ Baptist Church in Detroit as well as the founder of the Benjamin E. Mays Male Academy, a kindergarten through grade five institution that was established as a step toward saving African American youth. We will also look at Reverend Johnny Youngblood's life-changing programs for black males. These men and the other brothers and sisters you will read about in the pages that follow are building institutions that will help turn the tide. They are saying, "This is what we have done, and you can do the same thing."

I strongly encourage you to use the models within these pages. But before you adapt any of these models to the specific needs of your church and community, and before you initiate any suggested solutions for the black family, *put on the full armor of God.* Ephesians 6:12–17 tells us, "We wrestle not against flesh and blood, but against principalities, against powers, against the rulers of the darkness of this world, against spiritual wickedness in high places." We need to put on the full armor of God — his Word. That means the African American family and any ministry addressing its needs must have in hand the only weapon that can battle the schemes of Satan to destroy both family and ministry. The Word of God is both the best offense and the best defense for the black family.

The Scriptures that follow describe the power of the Word and are some of the *foundation Scriptures* for our solutions for the black family.

Psalm 119:11: "Thy word have I hid in mine heart, that I might not sin against thee." It is important that we are filled with the Word. When the Word is in our hearts, there is no turning back. We can stand on the truth of our Lord and not turn away from the course of ministry plans.

Luke 6:48: We need to dig deep and build our house on the Rock — Jesus — so that when floods come, the house will stand. Digging deep means that we pray without ceasing and study to show ourselves approved. Even when Satan gives us his best shot, if we have dug deep and put our house on the Rock, the house will stand!

Genesis 2:18: "The LORD God said, It is not good that the man should be alone; I will make him an help meet." Verse 24 continues, "Therefore shall a man leave his father and mother and shall cleave to his wife; they shall be one flesh." The Lord values family so much that he created that institution before all others.

Malachi 2:16: *God hates divorce.* Men and women are not to break apart what the Lord has joined together.

Colossians 3:18–20: The Lord gives strong counsel to families: "Wives submit yourselves unto your own husbands, as it is fit in the Lord. Husbands, love your wives, and be not bitter against them. Children, obey your parents in all things: for this is well pleasing unto the Lord." The Word of God joins husbands, wives, and children together in a unit of caring and trust toward one another.

Finally, we have an undeniable responsibility to the spiritual as well as the temporal well-being of our children. **Psalm 127:3:** "Children are an heritage of the LORD." They are a blessing from God and cannot be taken for granted. **Proverbs 22:6:** "Train up a child in the way he should go: and when he is old, he will not depart from it." We are preparing our children for the long haul. Their training is not just to get them through the next semester at school or past the teen years. We are to make sure that they will know how to stand and live for the Lord both now and when they are old and have raised up their own generation of offspring.

Deuteronomy 6:6–9: "And these words, which I command thee this day, shall be in thine heart: And thou shalt teach them diligently unto thy children, and shalt talk of them when thou sittest in thine house, and when thou walkest by the way, and when thou liest down, and when thou risest up. And thou shalt bind them for a sign upon thine hand, and they shall be as frontlets between thine eyes. And thou shalt write them upon the posts of thy house, and on thy gates."

Those of us who do not diligently teach the lessons of the Lord to our children and who do not "write them on our doorposts" help to assure that these children are destined to repeat historical mistakes over and over again. We cannot afford to lose one more child to ignorance.

Solutions for the African American family are rooted in knowing — and passing on to the next generation — these truths of the Word. We must heed the Lord's warnings about divorce and family life. We must live out our family unity by doing something as basic as having a meal together. We need to discuss at the dinner table our African American heritage — our strengths and our future. We must pass on to our children the spiritual and cultural lessons that will prepare them to do battle against those forces that would seek to cripple and destroy. These are some of the solutions for the black family. They will allow us to build a stronger tomorrow not only for our children but for our children's children throughout the next millennium.

PREFACE

How to Use This Book

Building Up Zion's Walls: Ministry for Empowering the African American Family is a direct outgrowth of the 1997 National African American Family Ministry Conference held in Detroit. It is a *training manual* based in large part on the materials presented by nationally renowned experts in topics that directly impact the quality of African American family life. The book is to be used by both clergy and lay leaders as they build ministries intended to strengthen today's families.

The book's format is designed so that readers can select as needed chapter topics that address the specific concerns of their congregation and the surrounding community. Thus, the chapters may be read in any order. The book is to be used as a working document to formulate programs in any of the specific areas discussed within its pages.

Used in this way, this book provides vital information that clergy and lay workers can utilize to dramatically affect the prosperity and well-being of the African American family well into the twenty-first century.

CHAPTER ONE

Reaching Black Males

Up Front

"...*Male and female he created them.*" Most of us have either heard or read this statement from Genesis 1:27 many times since our days as children in Sunday school and Vacation Bible School. The truth to these words is so obvious that we are inclined to dismiss their importance to us and their impact on us. Look at them again. Male and female God created them — male and female. From the time of creation an inextricable bond has existed between the two sexes. Although the two can exist separately, they were created to coexist. Furthermore, this coexistence is part of the image of God, as we read in this same verse. We can look at the union of a man and woman and know that by a God-driven power we are looking into the face of God.

The New Testament speaks of the "mystery" of the male and female union. Not only were the genders created to coexist, but Ephesians 5:31–32 quotes the book of Genesis in saying that in marriage the "two shall be one flesh." Of course this is a mystery. No other union in the world can demonstrate such a transformation. Even children, though carried in a mother's womb, are brought forth into the world to exist on their own. In verses 22–33 the apostle Paul, speaking of the sacred nature of the relationship between a husband and wife, likens it to the relationship between Christ and the church. We read, "as Christ is the head of the church," "as the church is subject to Christ," "as Christ also loved the church, and gave himself up for it." The necessity of the coexistence of Christ and the church mirrors the necessity of the coexistence of male and female.

What does that teach us? For the church on earth to function as God intends, the relationship between men and women must function as God intends. Just as the church cannot exist without Christ as the head, so the church cannot exist without the model of male and female coexisting and, in the sanctity of marriage, becoming one flesh. In other words, the church is not complete if there is an imbalance of men and women. They must coexist.

Unfortunately, most of our churches today are not representative of God's plan. The female presence, except in certain ministerial offices, is predominant. The male presence is sporadic, inconsistent, and, where it does occur, underutilized. This is as true in the African American church as it is anywhere else.

If the black church is to move forward and claim its rightful place as a driving force in the next millennium — particularly in its ministry to the African American family — something must be done to increase the number of black males in our congregations today.

In this chapter we will consider the impact a weak male presence in the church has on the African American church and family. We will look at methods and models that can lessen or even remedy the severity of this situation. We will consider how we can reach black males and thereby strengthen the capacity of the church to reflect God's image.

Think about It

Take a few minutes to write in the space provided below some ways in which:

- your church has developed ministries and programs to reach black males
- your church has nurtured and maintained the male presence it already has
- your church could improve the rapport it maintains with black males in the congregation and community

____

____

____

____

____

List new programs and ministries that could be implemented by your church to attract and maintain the black male presence in your congregation.

Focus

Seminaries do not adequately prepare students who graduate from degree programs to reach out into the community surrounding their church and bring in black males. Yes, there are seminars and practicums on evangelism and church planting. There is also a strong focus on ministering to and counseling parishioners with family crisis issues. Some seminaries are very concerned with the family. But if as described in Ephesians 5:22–33 the husband is to love the wife as Christ loved the church, then the husband can only learn that specific type of love when he is actively involved in a church that provides such a model for him to follow. How can we have even more thriving Christian African American families if we do not have more men in the church being nurtured, raised up, baptized, and then sent out into the community to see that other men have this same training?

The African American church has a biblical mandate to actively recruit and retain black men. The church of the twenty-first century demands nothing less.

One of the most powerful and empowering ministries that enjoys phenomenal success in reaching and retaining African American males for the church today is led by Rev. Johnny Youngblood, D.Min., pastor of St. Paul Community Baptist Church in Brooklyn, New York. A major workshop presenter at the African American Family Ministry Conference, Youngblood has accepted a spiritual mandate to bring more African American males back into the church and raise them up to be the Christian leaders of the next millennium. His methods are practical; the results are inspiring. The next sections of this chapter present what Youngblood's church has done, how they have done it, and how you can obtain similar results in your congregation.

The Word

No ministry can bear fruit and succeed unless it is rooted in the truth of the Scriptures. Youngblood's ministry is no exception. A wide variety of Bible passages serve as the basis for his vision and as proof of the validity of the steps he has taken in building this outreach ministry to black males.

As a basis for his faith in stepping out on untried waters in his mission to reach black males, Youngblood relies on Joshua 3. In that chapter the Israelites are instructed to cross the Jordan River. This crossing is different from the crossing of the Red Sea when Moses had led the people. At that time Moses had held out his staff, the waters had parted, and the people had crossed over on dry ground. Now the people are instructed to follow the priests who carry the ark of the covenant. When the priests come to the overflowing banks of the Jordan River, they are told to stand in the water; and at that point the waters of the Jordan will be cut off. The priests obey, and with the people of Israel close behind them, they stand in the water. At that point the waters of the Jordan stop flowing and the people cross over on dry ground.

The command to "stand in the water" is a command to "go on and start your ministry"; the Lord will bless what you have started and make a way for your plans. The command is to "go and get your feet wet." Do not wait for a perfect vision explaining every step that you will take to get the job done. Just stand in the water, and the waters will stop flowing long enough to allow you to walk on dry ground as you cross over to the other side of the river. The command is to *do something!*

Youngblood also relies on the truth in some familiar biblical passages that show that Jesus did not have a problem getting men to follow him. Jesus just said the word and men were willing to leave their livelihoods and financial security — all that they stood for as breadwinners in a household — and follow him. In Mark 1:16–18 the Lord calls Simon Peter and Andrew, two brothers who are fishermen, and they leave their nets and follow him. Simon Peter is married and has family responsibilities, yet when Jesus calls he answers without a moment's hesitation. In verses 19–20 Jesus passes two more brothers who are working with their father. Jesus calls them, and they stop mending their fishing nets and follow him. They do not ask their father's permission or apologize to him for leaving the family business on such short notice. They simply hear Jesus' call and follow him. Then in Mark 2:14 Jesus calls Levi the tax collector. Levi closes his tax books, puts down his stylus, and follows Jesus. The "Guideposts" section below will shed some light on why our Lord was able to elicit such responses from responsible working men and how Youngblood uses that insight to reach black males.

Finally, to confirm the need for men to work with men, and in particular fathers with sons, Youngblood examines Mark 9:17–24. Initially, the father is bringing his son, who is possessed with an evil spirit, to Jesus to be healed. However, upon meeting the Lord, he too seeks Jesus' touch. In verse 22 the father says, "Have compassion on *us,* and help *us*" (my emphasis). Somehow, in seeking Jesus for his son, the father realizes that they are on this journey toward healing together. There will be no healing from Jesus unless the father accepts his spiritual connection with his son. Then, at the point of healing, Jesus tells him that all things — even healing — are possible for those who believe. What does the father reply? "I believe; help my unbelief." "*My* unbelief." The father who initially only brought his son to Jesus to be healed now accepts his position as the main connection between Jesus and his son's healing. As head of the household, and as father to the son, if he believes, the son will be healed.

What a powerful lesson! If the connection between a father and the spiritual healing of his family is that strong, then we must not fail to lose another moment in bringing every man into the church for Christ!

Even these few passages show how the Bible supports, even mandates, the development of an effective ministry for reaching black males. Men have a biblically supported purpose to fulfill in completing the work of the Kingdom here on earth.

Guideposts

"Follow me, and I will make you fishers of men." With these few words in Mark 1:17 (NIV), Jesus gathers the first of his twelve disciples. How does he do it? Jesus offers them something to do, and the offer intrigues them. They already know about catching fish: they know all about repairing nets; they know the best time of day to cast their nets into the water; they know how much to expect from the market when they return with a load of fish. They know how much profit to put into boat repairs, how much to set aside for times when the catch comes up short, and how much to take home to support their families. But this idea — to be fishers of *men* — intrigues them. This is work they have never done before. The call from the Master is irresistible and even captivating!

This same call to be fishers of men is what sustains Youngblood's outreach ministry for black males in his surrounding community. Youngblood goes beyond the traditional male church roles of deacon and usher. There is a place for them, to be sure, and their importance in the church cannot be denigrated. However, utilizing men's talents in primarily these two areas means that there are a lot of other areas where talents are either being underutilized or ignored altogether. Outlets must be provided for the wells of creativity waiting to be tapped for the Christian kingdom. The question becomes, then, what would arouse the desire to use those talents for Christ?

Youngblood's answer is, "Give the brothers something else to do." It is that simple. Start by recognizing the men who are already in your congregation. Have them stand up during the Sunday service. Acknowledge them, thank them for their presence, encourage them to come back, and invite them to share with you what they are looking for from the church.

Next, hold weekly men's meetings. At Youngblood's church these gatherings are held on the same evening each week for no more than one and a half hours. The consistent day and time are maintained out of respect for the many demands already being made on men's time. To help break down any barriers that might keep them from relating on a man-to-man basis, the pastor should dress casually, even in a jogging suit and running shoes. There should be no visible obstacles between the pastor and the men. In this way the message being conveyed by the pastor to the men is that they are gathered together as men on equal footing with similar needs, desires, goals, and problems.

Another means of developing camaraderie in these weekly men's meetings is through something Youngblood calls "rounds." Each brother in attendance introduces himself and shares something about his identity; if he has a nickname, he is encouraged to share that also. Knowing the nickname can be important because it tells you something about their identification in the family and the community. When you can greet that brother and actually use his nickname, the two of you can share a new comfort level together.

With the casual dress and the maintenance of rounds, relationships are built. These men's meetings become part fraternity meeting and part therapy session. And the Bible study portions have not even started yet! There is plenty of time for Bible study. By rushing right into the Bible study portion of the men's meetings, some serious problems that some of these men may have with the Bible are often not recognized: problems with God and with Jesus. These problems must not be treated lightly. Some brothers may have trouble with what they have been told is the ethnicity of Jesus—blond hair and blue eyes. Pastors have to be sensitive to this fact and understand that racism and white supremacy is a factor in their perception of the Bible whether the brothers tell you so or not. The bottom line is that Jesus Christ was a black man. The Bible tells us that his hair was like lamb's wool (Revelation 1:14, KJV; cf. Daniel 7:9). He was from the Semitic portion of the world and had brown skin and crinkly hair. Once the men realize this and are able to deal with the perceptions that have kept them from being willing to open a Bible and really learn from it, then Bible studies can begin during the men's meetings.

Once the men start coming, in addition to giving them something to do, they have to feel as if they have some power. Not all of it has to be planned out ahead of time. Some of these programs evolve as pastors work with the men and put their feet in the water as in Joshua 3. One of these kinds of serendipitous programs is described by Youngblood as he relates the way the men in his congregation began to police their own community. It started when one of the young brothers from the church was cleaning up around the outside of the building and a drug dealer told him that he had to get off the dealer's territory. The youngster told the pastor. Youngblood gathered every man he could find — about twenty-five — and went out and confronted the drug dealer. They told him that *he*, not the young brother, would have to go. The drug dealer left.

The next morning, after service had begun, Youngblood told the women to remain at the church and pray. He gathered all of the men who were in the service and took them outside. Other men from the street joined them when they witnessed this force of black, Christian men. Youngblood led them into each local store that was suspected of dealing drugs and confronted the proprietors; with this huge force of men behind him, he told them that they would have to immediately stop dealing drugs. The brothers were amazed at the power they possessed. When they walked back to church, every man felt bigger, more powerful. This was something that the men had to do by themselves to feel the force of what they could do as a collective unit.

Power can be shared within the structure of the church. In Youngblood's congregation the deacons have been renamed elders and their job descriptions have been changed. They are now like a board of directors and serve as leaders in every area of the church. In addition, the elders never present anything to the congregation to be voted on that does not have their unanimous approval. In this way the power of these elders resonates throughout the entire church.

Regarding outreach to young boys, Youngblood works with the elementary school that was started by his church. Because most of his staff at the school — the principal, administrator, and faculty — are female, he recruits men from the congregation to go to the school, show a male presence, and have male input. Most of the volunteers are retired men from his church because they are the ones who have time to interact with the youngsters during school hours. These volunteers are trained by the Christian brother who initiated the program.

Another popular outreach vehicle for Youngblood's church is the annual Resurrection Sunday Parade. Of nearly two thousand people in the parade, almost half are men. Each year men from the community come from the parade into the church because they see for themselves that a large body of *men* is active in the church.

Another member of his church works for the Internal Revenue Service. Each year he trains men at the church to help members and the community with their taxes.

Also, the men play basketball and handball and go to the gym together. They have all-male retreats and a male round up with a focus on youngsters in the church and community.

Reaching black males for the church is a powerful mission. The number and content of creative programs intended to attract men to the church is limited only by your own instinctive feel for the needs and talents in your congregation and the surrounding community. Step into the water and be confident in your ability to offer the men in your community a life based on the resurrection power that comes only from faith in Jesus Christ.

Q & A

Question: Besides nicknames, what else is asked during “rounds” in the men’s meetings?

Answer: Any of their history regarding church attendance, such as what type of church they attended as a child and whether their mother and father attended church. Once they start talking about themselves, try to remember as much as you can without having to write anything down.

Question: When are actual Bible studies added to the men’s meeting?

Answer: Full Bible studies are added gradually. They are interspersed throughout what is, as was said above, part fraternity meeting, part therapy session. So much is happening in the men’s lives — getting fired, wives threatening to leave them, kids needing tutoring to keep up at school — that you can add Bible study to the meetings without it actually having to be a Bible study.

Question: Do men work in the church before they have accepted Christ?

Answer: Yes, definitely. The only qualification is that they must work with members. They can be a part of any group, but they cannot be a leader of the group before they have accepted Christ and become a member.

Question: If a woman is in charge of pastoral care, what do we do if a man comes to us for direction?

Answer: Listen but do not advise. Then be resourceful. Direct them to another man who can actually advise them. Of course, men are willing to listen to women, but they are led by women so much: school teachers, female heads of house, even their wives! They need to be directed to have relationships with other men.

Question: In building up all of this interest in male ministry, aren't women being ignored?

Answer: Definitely not! If women want more responsible husbands, it is the church's duty to help the men become more responsible. If women give birth to boys, it is the church's responsibility to help the women raise those boys. The church should be involved in changing lives, male and female. But there is such a dire need out in the community right now for effective Christian male leadership that even if a church's focus becomes directed more toward a men's ministry, the women will not be left out; they will benefit because the total life of the community will be enhanced by the changed lives of the men.

Highlights

Below are some of this chapter's main points to consider. After this list, be sure to include other points that are important to you.

- The African American church has a biblical mandate to actively recruit and retain black men.
- The command from Joshua 3 is to "go and get your feet wet." In other words, *do something* — start your male ministry, and the Lord will bless your work.
- Jesus never had a problem getting men because he offered them *something to do.*

- Recognize the men who are already in your congregation.
- Weekly men's meetings help men feel comfortable in the church setting.
- During the men's meeting, "rounds" help the men become more comfortable with the pastor and with each other.
- Male members have to feel that they have power within the ministry with programs such as policing their own neighborhoods.
-
-
-
-
-

Think about It – Again

In light of what has been presented in this chapter, consider again what new programs and ministries could be implemented by your church to attract and maintain the black male presence in your congregation.

___

___

___

___

___

___

___

___

___

___

CHAPTER TWO

Faith Development in the Family

Up Front

God's mandate in Deuteronomy 6:5–7 is clear: "Thou shalt love the LORD thy God with all thine heart, and with all thy soul, and with all thy might. And these words, which I command thee this day, shall be in thine heart: And thou shalt teach them diligently unto thy children, and shalt talk of them when thou sittest in thine house, and when thou walkest by the way, and when thou liest down, and when thou risest up."

The Lord's instructions to parents are explicit. We have a duty to teach our children the ways of the Lord *in our own homes.* Of course, church attendance, Sunday school, children's church, and Christian youth groups all are important. Each has its place in the nurture, development, and socialization of our children and teens. But the home makes an indelible mark on them. Even if later in life our children momentarily turn away from our counsel and the teachings we have laid before them, they will be inclined to return to the guidelines of their home base.

At home children learn how to live, and they learn what it means to be connected within a family. They watch us eat, sleep, talk, laugh, and cry. They watch how we react to pain and sorrow as well as pleasure and joy. They learn how to maintain good health by seeing us prepare healthy meals and take them to the doctor's office for checkups. They learn to run a household by watching us maintain the yard, paint the house, stock the shelves with groceries, and pay our utility bills on time.

Now, if they can learn by our example all of these things that are necessary to a good and balanced life but that are not specifically Christian in and of themselves, how much more will they learn the things of the Lord from us by watching what we do and how we do it?

To make our homes places where our children will learn of the ways of the Lord, they must hear us speaking of the goodness of God in our daily conversations. They must not think that the only time we invoke the Lord's name is at church or when there is a crisis at home and we have nowhere else to turn. They must know that Jesus is the Lord of our lives even in the mundane routine of daily family life. For example, let them see that we joyfully maintain our yards or enjoy taking the family for a walk through the park because we are grateful for all of God's creation. Let them know that we are truly thankful for the food we eat because it is part of the Lord's bounty. Tell them that we gather together for prayer as a family before meals because the Lord tells us that where two or more are gathered in his name, he is there in the midst of them.

Developing a family lifestyle in which we go one step further and immerse our children in the Word, teach them the meaning of Scriptures, show them how we live by the Word, and apply it to our daily lives requires even greater diligence and commitment on our part.

Helping us to establish and maintain this scripturally mandated commitment to the faith development of our children and families are two presenters from the African American Family Ministry Conference — Rev. Dr. Robert and Mrs. Marquita Stephens. Their desire is to equip our families to take their rightful places in God's plan of redemption for all of humankind. This chapter introduces effective ways to live out the mandate of responsibility from Deuteronomy 6:5–7 both in our families and in our homes.

Think about It

Take a few minutes to write in the space provided below some ways in which:

- your church has developed ministries and programs to strengthen families through faith development in the home

- your church supports parents in their quest to raise children in the knowledge, love, and discipline of the Lord
- your church helps and encourages parents and guardians in their quest to lead Christ-centered lives as an example for their children

Considering the specific needs of the families in your church and the surrounding community, list any new programs and ministries that could be implemented by your church that would better nurture their faith development.

Focus

As we approach the twenty-first century, many societal ills that we thought would be lessened if not altogether eradicated over time have proven to be problems with immense staying power. Racism, sexually transmitted diseases, day care transmitted diseases, teenage pregnancy, high infant mortality rates, homelessness — these social ills have impacted the very fiber of American society in ways that make it virtually impossible to enter the new century with a clean slate. We must find ways to deal with these issues, and quickly, if the next millennium is to chart its own course and not be defined by the litany of previous mistakes and dilemmas.

"What do we do?" is a question posed not only by social scientists and theologians as they ponder the accumulated ramifications of hundreds of years of culturally sanctioned sin and societal neglect, but also by parents who are struggling to raise children in this current era. Parents must protect their young children from the effects of societal ills. Then, as these same children mature, parents must train them in a way that will prevent them from manifesting these sins.

What do we do? One very effective response (and the one that is the focus of this chapter) is tied to a process of faith development in the family. And, although it is a lifestyle that encompasses the entire family — parents, guardians, children, and extended family — the primary focus is on the children. The children must be taught and made ready to do battle against the symptoms of sin that are rampant in our society. The way they are taught this is through a systematic program of Bible-based teaching and sharing by the parents.

One particular method of teaching our children within the family structure, which we will share later, has been developed by Dr. and Mrs. Stephens and was presented to the participants of the National African American Family Ministry Conference. Their particular focus is on the African American family and African American children. The primary purpose behind the Stephenses' presentation was not so much to provide a concrete program to be followed by every church (each congregation must assess the needs of its membership and the surrounding community and tailor the program to fit those particular needs), but to convince church leaders of the crucial need for such a program of faith development in the family and motivate them to implement such a program in their church.

The Stephenses describe the three functions of the family as (1) providing mutual support for the adult members, (2) providing nurturing protection for the children, and (3) providing the type of support for the children that will bring them to the age of accountability.

The age of accountability is a very important concept. Where for some time it represented the age when older teenagers and young adults were able to generate income and become responsible for their own actions, the whole notion of accountability is now shifting to encompass younger age groups as during the industrial revolution when child labor abuses were common. This shift is more acute for many African American children than for the majority of white American children. Certain dynamics of our American culture dictate that reality. Whereas for the middle class and the privileged the age of accountability occurs after they attend school and are trained to earn a livelihood, for far too many poor inner-city youngsters the age of accountability has dropped to the early teens, when they can be pulled into the criminal justice system and tried as adults. The majority of these youths do not have hope for or access to opportunities for higher education and acceptable livelihoods. Unfortunately, the reality of our urban centers and the prevalence of the drug culture dictate that even if children are not predisposed to be attracted to or pulled into the criminal, underworld culture, they may be unwittingly dragged into the tangles of the criminal justice system by something as simple as being at the wrong place at the wrong time. The reality of a reduced age of accountability will be forced upon them before they are ready.

In addition, the prevalent cultural references to sexual promiscuity and immorality through dress, language, and entertainment are exposing children of all socioeconomic levels to a value system that is in direct opposition to the values of a nurturing Christian family.

The program devised by the Stephenses addresses these issues. It provides a model for Christian families to use in dealing with the hard-core matters that affect today's families while it brings our children to the age of accountability in such a way that they are not victimized by the forces of evil in our society.

The Word

The Stephenses provide biblical support for the following three faith claims:

1. Genesis 6:1–6: Our society and culture are the vehicles through which evil is expressed by humanity.
2. Matthew 2:1–23: The family that is functioning within the bounds of Christian faith is better able to mitigate the forces of evil in our society.
3. Ephesians 5–6: The family is God's instrument in the plan of redemption that sets humans free from the entrapment of evil.

The opening chapters of the book of Genesis describe the creation, the first family, enmity against God and each other within that first family, and the generational nature of that enmity as the first children rise up against one another. As we look farther down the timespan at Genesis 6:1–6, however, we see the emergence of culture and society—and it is not a pretty sight. We see evil revealing itself in the midst of this society. In fact, the Lord "saw that the wickedness of man was great in the earth, and that every imagination of the thoughts of his heart was only evil continually." There was so much evil in the hearts of the people and expressed through the culture that the Lord decided to destroy everyone and everything. Then and now evil expresses itself through culture and society.

Fortunately, the Bible shows us the way to lessen the effect of this evil in society. We see in Matthew 2:1–23 that after Jesus' birth, evil manifested itself through the person of Herod, who wanted to kill the child Jesus. To protect the child, the angel of the Lord spoke to Joseph in a dream and told him to take Jesus and Mary to Egypt and stay there until it was safe to return. Faithful to God and wanting to raise his family within the boundaries of his faith, Joseph obeyed the Lord's command. Evil still worked in Bethlehem society as Herod ordered the murder of all children two years old and under. Joseph, however, bypassed that evil for the sake of his family by following the Lord's word. The family unit, with Joseph as the head, was functioning as a united, faith-based entity and was able to respond to save itself from the impending crisis. As Christian families today, and as the adult leaders of those families, we will not eradicate evil; but we can mitigate the influence of society's evil upon our families by obeying the Lord's commands and letting him guide our actions in our families.

The Letter of Ephesians was written largely in response to a wonderful phenomenon that was taking place in Ephesus — namely, huge numbers of people were becoming Christians. In many cases, however, those who were converted were still attracted to or were active participants in the cultural practices of the dominant society. Those practices — such as the worship of false gods, idol making, and even temple prostitution — were keeping some recent believers from enjoying the full measure of the fruit of their faith in Christ. Paul's message to the Ephesian believers is clearly meant to guide them toward the implementation of a Christian lifestyle that will lead them away from the evils of their culture. Paul teaches them how to act in the family unit so that the Christian lifestyle can firmly take root.

Ephesians 5–6 gives detailed instructions to husbands, wives, and children on creating a family that by its very makeup allows its members to live for Christ and not for the dominant culture:

- husbands, love your wives *as Christ loved the church*
- men, love your wives as you love your own body
- wives, submit yourselves to your husbands, *as unto the Lord*
- children, *obey* your parents
- children, *honor* your mother and father

After his message to families, Paul exhorts them to, "be strong in the Lord and in the power of his might" and to "put on the whole armor of God" in order to withstand the lure of society and its evils. The family that is rooted in Christ can better withstand the lure and presence of evil.

Guideposts

Programs based on the scriptural mandates listed above as well as on the need to equip our families — especially our children — with specific tools to do battle against the forces of evil in society can be initiated by the church but carried out in the home. Rev. and Mrs. Stephens have devised a church-initiated ministry program of Bible reflection designed to promote faith development in the family. This program readily responds to the dilemma of transmitting the tenets of our faith from one generation to the next. It equips parents with the tools necessary to make their children "spiritually ready" as they approach the age of accountability. It also prepares our families to take the front-line position in our spiritual battle against the forces of evil rooted in our society. They will be so attuned to the leading of the Lord that when he gives direction, these families will be prepared to move with him against the dictates of the culture.

Since this program takes place once a week in the home, it can be incorporated easily into the routine of any family. It serves three purposes essential to a family ministry: (1) it provides mutual support for the adult members in the family, (2) it provides nurturing and protecting support for the children, and (3) it provides a spiritual foundation for the children in preparation for the demands of the age of accountability.

Since this Bible reflection program is initiated by the church, the church has a mandate to help its parishioners commit their time to the project. This can be done by presenting members with a contract or covenant that will ask each member to commit to meet together as a family each week for one hour of Bible reflection. Then the church, through a committee or the pastor, must follow up to see that the members keep the covenant. The church should stress that the best way to show dedication to the project is to set aside a specific period of time each week for the Bible reflection. Another strong point worth emphasizing is that in setting aside time for each other in the family, we are also setting aside time for God, who is there in the midst of them.

In addition to each family signing the covenant for weekly Bible reflection in the home, the church must, in a program of several sessions, train the heads of families to embrace the Scriptures in preparation for this Bible reflection. The church must not present the Bible reflection as another "Bible study" program, but rather as an exciting opportunity to use the Scriptures as a tool for discerning God's will for each family and for providing help and encouragement for each particular circumstance.

In these preparatory sessions, heads of families will be taught to "reflect" on the status of their family and on their particular needs and goals. They will be taught how to read the Bible with an eye toward the needs of their family as they negotiate their place in life and society and prepare their children to enter the age of accountability. They will be encouraged to take part in "contextual analysis," in which they will put themselves in the shoes of such biblical family members as Sarah, Abraham, Isaac, Rebecca, Ruth, Boaz, Eli, Mary, Joseph, Elizabeth, Joanna, Lydia, the Roman centurion, Paul, and Silas, and ask, "How does this work for me and my family? How can I gain understanding from the dynamics of this biblical family for help and guidance in our particular circumstance?" Pastors and lay leaders, knowing their particular congregations and communities, must sit down and devise training programs that will be beneficial for handling the kinds of issues confronting their church families.

Families must be shown how to "critique" the prevailing culture for their children and not just throw up their hands in helpless frustration. Families must be given assistance in using the Bible to help their children understand how to avoid pitfalls that are waiting to engulf them as they grow and mature. Families must be encouraged to bring up such topics as choosing an appropriate mate; Christian dating; materialism; and sexually explicit music, movies, and other entertainment. These hours of Bible reflection must be times when families can wrestle with the issues that concern them with their own particular needs in mind. They must be reminded that there is no issue ready to confront them that the Bible does not address in some form that is helpful to their situation.

The church must present the Bible as a readily available, *living* manual for coping with the societal issues that intrude upon today's family. It is a personal "fix-it" tool as well as a source of preventative medicine. It should not only be relied upon as a crutch when we are down but as a guide to avoiding the many pitfalls lurking throughout society and the world.

Once the family has signed the covenant and the head of the household has attended the training sessions, the family is ready to begin the weekly Bible reflection hours. Initially, church members will undoubtedly inundate the pastor with questions indicating a need for support and encouragement in this venture. Pastors and other lay leaders should remember, however, that one main objective of the church is to equip the congregation to share in the priesthood of all believers. Families can take control of the spiritual direction of their marriages and their children. Through weekly study of the Scriptures, families can prepare their children to enter the age of accountability ready to wage spiritual warfare against the forces of evil in society. Families can connect with the Scriptures in a way that allows them to get instruction pertinent to their particular situations. But these same families must be given help and encouragement every step of the way as they negotiate what will probably be very foreign territory for them during this weekly hour of Bible reflection and exploration. The pastor's door must always be open to them; help must always be given freely to these families as they begin their adventure in family faith development.

Another component of the churches' mission for family faith development is to provide a structure where, the Stephenses say, "males can learn to be males and females can learn to be females." Believing that slavery has created a huge distortion in the way African American men and women relate to one another, the Stephenses have devised two gender-specific programs. The goal of these programs is to help men and women mature in their development to such an extent that they will be able to function in mutually supportive relationships.

The first of these programs is called the African American Male Empowerment Network. In this network men look at issues that can cause them to believe that they are supposed to be unemotional and detached yet competitive and against others. They also try to help men recognize the incidents in their lives when they injure and hurt those to whom they are closest — times when even their spouse becomes their enemy.

The second program is called Women of Faith. In this group women, and in particular African American women, are invited to identify destructive influences in their lives. They are encouraged to empower themselves to break out of the socialization that causes them to choose to live in or accept subservient roles or abusive conditions in a relationship.

In both groups the men and women are advised to seek a "spiritual counselor," someone who understands psychological methods yet can also work with clients in intensifying their connection with God.

The mission of all of these programs is to strengthen men, women, and families in ways that will enable them to withstand the forces of evil that are prevalent in our society. Weekly family Bible reflections, male empowerment networks, and women's faith groups form a cohesive unit; they are a Christ-centered shield to help us exist in the presence of evil while at the same time maintaining our Christian integrity.

Q & A

Question: I'm single. How am I supposed to be a part of a weekly Bible reflection program?

Answer: Whether you are part of a two-parent family, a single-parent household, or live alone as a single individual, the purpose of the weekly Bible reflection hour — to help you maintain Christian faith development in the home — applies to you. Use that special hour to reflect on what is going on in the culture and how it affects you. Choose Scripture passages that can help you maintain your anchor in Christ as you live your daily life.

Question: How do we keep our young children interested in the Bible reflection hour week after week?

Answer: Try having a special dessert after the weekly session; this will give the kids something to look forward to. Also, have a time of singing before the start of each week's session. Choose Christian songs that they are already familiar with and that are fun to sing. Be sure to take your cue from your children. If there is something that goes on during a certain week that they seem to particularly enjoy, do that activity more often. Ask for their input; make this a time when the family is truly united around the goal of faith development.

Question: I've never read or studied the Bible as much as I should. Now how am I supposed to lead my family in looking at the Scriptures each week?

Answer: One of the best places to get started in family Bible reflections is the book of Proverbs. The verses are short and sweet and are filled with principles for negotiating a Christian life in the midst of a sick and perverse society — living as a wise man or wise woman, controlling anger, controlling the tongue, despising greed, controlling desire, living justly — the list goes on. Your comfort level with Bible reflections will grow the more you immerse yourself in the Proverbs.

Highlights

These are some of the main points to remember from this chapter. After reading this list, be sure to include other points that are of interest of you.

- We have a duty to teach our children the ways of the Lord in our own homes.
- Faith development in the family requires that the entire family — especially the children — be taught and made ready to do battle against the symptoms of sin that are rampant in our society.
- Evil expresses itself through culture and society.
- The family that is rooted in Christ can better withstand the lure and presence of evil.
- A church-initiated ministry program of weekly Bible reflection in the family promotes family faith development and provides family members with defenses against cultural evil.
- The church must train the heads of families to embrace and explore the Scriptures in preparation for family Bible reflection.
- This time of Bible reflection creates a spiritual foundation for children in preparation for the demands of the age of accountability.
- During these weekly sessions, families should be taught how to critique the prevailing culture in light of the values learned in the Bible reflections.
-
-
-
-
-

Think about It – Again

In light of what has been presented in this chapter, consider again what new programs and ministries could be implemented by your church to begin a program of faith development in the families of your congregation.

CHAPTER THREE

Models for Youth Ministry

Up Front

Even in Jesus' time children were considered to be lower-class citizens. Once when Jesus was teaching the people, some in the crowd brought their children to him so that he could touch them. These were parents like you and me, and they just wanted their children to be blessed by Jesus. But the disciples would not hear of it. Thinking they were protecting Jesus' precious time, they soundly rebuked the parents for bringing their children to Jesus.

"Jesus is a very busy man," the disciples said to the parents in the crowd. "He doesn't have time to touch every little kid who comes along. Go on, now! Move it!"

Jesus heard the talk that was going on behind him and said, "Suffer the little children to come unto me, and forbid them not: for of such is the kingdom of God" (Mark 10:14,16). Jesus turned what was a moment of expediency for the disciples into a teaching moment for them and the crowd. He continued, "Whosoever shall not receive the kingdom of God as a little child, he shall not enter therein. And he took them up in his arms, put his hands upon them, and blessed them."

Jesus — try to see the moment — not only spoke to the children but took them in his arms, held them, hugged them, and blessed them. He took them from the point of being rebuked and pushed away by the disciples to being held and blessed by the Savior of humanity. The disciples must have stood there with their mouths hanging open. The children's parents were probably just as astounded. Had not their children only a few moments ago been sent scurrying back into the crowd? And now Jesus, this new teacher — some even believing him to be the Son of God — was gathering their children to his bosom. He was doing all that he could to show the children, their parents, the disciples, the Pharisees, and the crowd pressing around him that he loved these children and that they were the most important people in the world to him.

What do we say to that? Let us think about how we treat our own children — with a hug and a blessing or a quick look up from the computer screen and a grunt? When was the last time we told them we loved them? When was the last time we declined an offer to play golf so that we could take a bike ride around the neighborhood with them? Do we see children as representatives of the kingdom of God and as examples of what it takes to get closer to God or as pests and nuisances?

Think about the atmosphere in our churches. Are we any more welcoming of children now than Jesus' disciples were two thousand years ago? Have we learned anything at all from this lesson? Do we sit down and actually ask our youth what *we* can do for *them?* Do we mentor them or offer them tutoring? Do we let them sing their kind of gospel/rap music in church? Do we allow them the freedom to talk their own language in the fellowship hall, and are we then willing to sit with them and learn that language so that we can maintain open lines of communication? The young people who do come to our churches need to be made to feel as if they are a part of the life and vitality of the church and not as objects to be regarded with suspicion.

The lack of meaningful numbers of young people in most of today's congregations speaks of our inability to understand Jesus' simple message to the disciples, the crowd, and us: children represent the kingdom of heaven. Their presence is good, desirable, and necessary in order to comprehend something as basic to our faith as entering the kingdom of heaven. We need our youth. Our churches need our youth. We need to follow Jesus' example by reaching out and welcoming our children back into our hearts — and churches — with open arms and a blessing.

Think about It

In the space provided below, list the ways in which your congregation has truly welcomed young people to the church and made a way for them to maintain a meaningful presence in the life of the church.

-
-
-
-
-

List any new programs that could be initiated to give young people a more meaningful place in the life of the church.

-
-
-
-
-

Focus

"The African American church is an unfriendly place for young people." This statement was made by a pastor whose church has one of the most dynamic programs for young people in the United States, Rev. Dr. DeForest ("Buster") Soaries. The impact of this statement cannot be taken lightly, for its truth is staring us squarely in the face.

Soaries compares the church attendance of African American youth one or two generations ago with that of African American youths' church attendance today. Previously, we went to church because our parents told us to go to church. The family, church, and neighborhood shaped our culture and social existence. Our world was built on the nature of the African American experience. Today, however, black youth in

Newark, New Jersey, have more in common with white youth in Butte, Montana, than they do with their own grandparents. The youth culture has gone through a dramatic metamorphosis. Whereas in our generation black youth listened to the Temptations and white youth listened to the Beatles, today both blacks and whites are listening to Snoop Dogg and Puff Daddy.

Ministry to youth today is cross-cultural ministry. We are trying to reach out and attract children and teens who are immersed in a new culture and a new language, and who embrace a totally new set of values. Our young people are different. They do not fear what we fear; they do not view as vulgar what we view as vulgar. Their core values are no longer the core values of our race. That is why, according to Soaries, "our 'good' girls get pregnant, our 'good' boys sell drugs, and our 'good' kids cuss each other out. If our approaches to our children are based upon the assumption that they will do what we did, then we will be talking on an AM frequency and they will be listening on an FM frequency." No meaningful communication will be occurring between our generation and our youth!

In most communities gangs have an easier time attracting our young people than do our churches, because gang members speak the same language, represent the same culture, wear the same clothes, and espouse similar values. If we were as willing to seek common ground, reach past all of the naysayers, and embrace our young people *as they are*, we would have no trouble attracting teens to the church. Ask the trustees to give up their seats and invite youth to the seats of honor in the front pews. Welcome teens with their baggy pants, dreadlocks, and pierced nostrils. Translate sermons so that they, too, can understand the Good News of a mighty, living God. When this happens, we will have young people packed into the aisles, jamming the narthex, and spilling out into the street!

In this chapter we will be introduced to the youth ministry of Dr. Buster Soaries. Take time to closely examine the ways in which his church has become sensitive to the needs of today's young people. Then be prepared to welcome a whole new generation of worshipers and Christian believers into your congregation!

The Word

In 1 Timothy 4:11–16, the apostle Paul exhorts Timothy:

> Let no man despise thy youth; but be thou an example of the believers, in word, in conversation, in charity, in spirit, in faith, in purity. Till I come, give attendance to reading, to exhortation, to doctrine. Neglect not the gift that is in thee, which was given thee by prophecy, with the laying on of the hands of the presbytery. Meditate upon these things; give thyself wholly to them; that thy profiting may appear to all. Take heed unto thyself, and unto the doctrine; continue in them: for in doing this thou shalt both save thyself, and them that hear thee.

As a young man, Soaries read these verses as a source of encouragement as he entered the uncharted realms of the pastoral ministry. He knew that even if older members in the church, more established ministers in town, or other people in "powerful" positions did not recognize him in his pastoral position, he was not to be discouraged. Then, after gaining experience in the ministry and with youth, Soaries began to turn the situation around. He wondered not so much why Timothy should be admonished not to get discouraged in the face of so much opposition to his youth but why Paul had to warn Timothy about these problems in the first place.

Soaries realized that then as now, there are some "misguided" people within the walls of the church who do not understand young people, do not want to understand young people, and will — wittingly or unwittingly — try to derail all or most of your attempts to reach out to and minister to the youth of the church and community.

Realizing this, and wearing the armor of the Spirit of God, Soaries has put together a youth program that can withstand the critique of both the young who do not want to enter through the church door, and the old who may not want these young people to enter through the church door either. Examine your current ministries and programs in light of what you read in the "Guideposts" section below. There you will find food for thought and plans for action for all churches who have a heart for the needs and salvation of our youth.

Guideposts

We will address some obstacles to an effective youth ministry before listing some of the solutions.

• *Parents.* Many parents are sick and in pain themselves (either emotionally, physically, or both). Added to their own personal problems are the needs and problems of their children, and there is not always enough — or any — support from the parents for what the church is trying to accomplish with young people.

• *Pastors.* Too many pastors do not have the interests of young people as a priority. They do not visit teen classes in Sunday school or stop by and have lunch with them at the local high school. They do not have a systematic way of staying in touch with these youngsters and assessing how the church might best address their needs.

• *Church youth leaders.* Unfortunately, some of these leaders may be working in the youth area of the church because they had difficulty in other areas of ministry. Be aware that some may have unresolved issues in their own lives, which will limit their effectiveness in youth ministry. The results can be devastating for both the young people and the future of the youth ministry in the church if a youth leader is ill equipped for the job.

The solutions, in spite of these obstacles, are quite basic and easy to implement for most congregations. First, we have to understand that effective youth ministry is effective family ministry. Healing has to take place at home between children and their parents. It is the church's responsibility to sponsor activities that will bring them together, teaching youth and their parents how to talk to one another and even have fun together.

Once we begin opening up the lines of communication, information will start to surface that is not always easy to handle. A teen may divulge in a youth encounter session that she has been abused by her father. Another may have a mother in prison whom she has not seen since she was a toddler. The church has to be prepared to step in and offer counseling services that will assist youngsters in dealing with such situations. The church has to offer services to the parents as well, or at least be in a position to make referrals to the appropriate agencies and groups who can provide help in these situations.

Youth ministry in isolation is dangerous as well as ineffective. A church must be serious about ministering to *families* if it is to have an effective ministry to children and teens. The church becomes an instrument of healing as well as mediation in facilitating the repair of fractured, broken, or dysfunctional relationships in families.

Next, in creating programs directed primarily for youth, Soaries has developed a series of priority areas that are evaluated each month for their effectiveness in the church's ministry to young people. These are:

- academic achievement
- spiritual growth
- cultural exposure
- family issues and development
- social development and civic consciousness
- economic development and entrepreneurship
- personal problems and access to appropriate resources
- recreation

The actual programs developed by each church for each of these areas will be determined by the specific needs of that church and the surrounding community. However, we will look in detail at one particular program at Soaries' church to determine how it functions and why it works.

Academic achievement. If we are serious about youth ministry, then a child who comes to church each week should be better off academically than the child who does not come to church. This does not happen automatically; a consistent approach and planning are vital.

First, Soaries' church has a youth board of directors that includes young people. It meets once each month to coordinate activities. It also evaluates the commitment and effectiveness of each of the church's programs as it relates to youth. Each youth program has a unified block of support. No one youth program operates in isolation; this is a team ministry. Representatives of the youth choir, junior usher board, junior missionaries, JAM (the actual youth ministry), tutoring program, and any others with an impact on youth meet together and place their agendas on the table. This insures that there are no duplications of programs, budgetary requests, or staff and volunteer needs. No group has a hidden program; each group knows the goals and needs of the others, and they can thereby work together to assure the success and efficacy of each of their projects in relation to the total youth ministry. This is planning in its truest sense!

To assure that no student falls through the cracks because he or she does not take part in the particular church youth program that monitors academic achievement and progress, *all* youth programs in the church monitor the academic achievement of their students. Each group looks at the report cards of its students at each marking period. And just in case a student is not involved in any program at the church, at the end of each quarter all students get a gift from the church for bringing their report cards to church on a designated Sunday. The pastor stops the regular service, the youth line up, and the pastor gives them gifts for bringing in their report cards. Each receives a gift no matter what his or her grades are; the important factor is that each students brings in the card and is thereby drawn into the loop. The church celebrates the achievement of *all* of the youth who bring in their cards.

If a student does not bring in his or her report card, the pastor calls the parent and asks permission to go to the school and see the child's grades there. This drives home to everyone the importance the church is placing on academic performance and excellence.

Any student who gets below a B in any subject is automatically assigned to a tutor. Thus, a functioning tutoring program must be in place. Each youth program must be vigilant in monitoring the academic progress of its students in order to make the appropriate tutoring referral.

This system for monitoring and assuring academic achievement can be used for all of the church youth programs. Planning and follow-up are essential.

Another essential component is maintaining a competent and committed contingent of volunteers. This takes place by training and recruiting people for bite-sized assignments and not lifelong pursuits. When the church approaches someone, that person is not offered an open-ended invitation to serve. Each person signs up for service for one year only. At the end of the year, that person's performance and personal situation are evaluated to determine whether he or she will be asked to remain for another year. If someone is doing a great job with the youth, he or she may be asked to continue for another year — or possibly not. Things change: volunteers marry, divorce, get pregnant, receive a promotion at work, change jobs. The person may be doing a wonderful job but may just be burned out. Any number of things can happen to impact a volunteer's ability to effectively operate within the constraints of the church's ministry to youth. This does not mean that if a volunteer is not asked to commit himself or herself for another year he or she will not be approached for service at another time. It just means that the one year of commitment is enough for the time being.

Once volunteers are recruited, they are trained. They learn what they must do and how they must do it. There must be quality control in the church, particularly in the areas of youth ministry. If, for instance, a volunteer math tutor learns that a student is addicted to crack cocaine, he knows where to refer the child within the church. The math tutor does not try to handle the drug problem himself.

The church thanks its youth volunteers and recognizes them for their efforts. When volunteers are given recognition for tasks that they have performed on behalf of youth, it is easier to get other volunteers to step forward, for they know that their work will be appreciated by the church.

Q & A

Question: Eight priority areas were listed for Rev. Soaries' youth ministry. Of these, which are the most important?

Answer: According to Rev. Soaries, his church's youth ministry has three main objectives — spiritual growth, economic empowerment, and academic excellence.

Question: In a major undertaking such as monitoring the academic achievement of the church youth by examining their report cards, how do you get started?

Answer: Try having a party and requiring a report card for admittance. Or sponsor a free trip to a theme park for students who present their report cards. Celebrate the participation and not necessarily the grades. All report cards are treated equally in public. Once the church reviews them, then it is determined who needs tutoring and who does not. Also, even if students do not need tutoring, they may still need help with time management. Students have to be made aware that this is an important commitment of the church and one that they are expected to take as seriously as the church does. To show how serious the church is about academic achievement, if a student does not show a report card or if once the student does, he or she does not accept tutoring, the student may not stay in the youth program he or she is involved in. This has never been a problem at Soaries' church because the youth want help. In fact, some youth know at the beginning of the school year in September that they will need help in a subject and do not wait for report card marking to ask for a tutor.

Highlights

These are some of the main points regarding youth ministry in this chapter. After reading this list, please include other points that are important for you and your church's youth program.

- The young people who do come to our churches need to be made to feel as if they are a part of the life and vitality of the church.
- Ministry to youth today is cross-cultural. We are trying to reach out to children and teens who are immersed in a new culture, a new language, and who embrace a totally new set of values.
- Effective youth ministry is effective family ministry.
- A consistent approach and good planning are vital to youth ministry.

- No one youth program operates in isolation. Youth programs work as a team.
- Another essential component to effective youth ministry is maintaining a competent and committed contingent of volunteers. This takes place by recruiting and training people for bite-sized assignments and not lifelong pursuits.
-
-
-
-
-

Think about It – Again

In light of what has been presented in this chapter, consider again what new programs and ministries your church could implement for a more effective youth ministry.

____

____

____

____

____

____

____

____

____

____

CHAPTER FOUR

Strengthening Communities through Economic Development

Up Front

Most of us are familiar with the parable of the talents. In this parable Jesus teaches his disciples about a man who was preparing to go on a long journey. He gathered his servants together and entrusted his worldly goods to them. To one he gave five talents, to another he gave two talents, and to the third he gave one talent. Then he left on his journey.

The one to whom the master left five talents invested them and earned five more talents. The one to whom the master left two talents also invested them and earned two more talents. The one to whom the master left one talent dug a hole in the ground and buried the talent.

After the master returned from his long journey, he summoned his servants to him. This is the conversation that followed between the master and his servants:

> The first servant greeted his master and said to him, "Master, I took the five talents you gave to me, invested them, and now have five more to give back to you."
>
> The master smiled at his servant and said, "You have done very well. Since you were so wise in handling a few things, I can trust you to handle many things. Come on down to the main house so that we can work together."

> The second servant bowed deeply before his master and said to him, "Master, you trusted two talents to my care. I also invested them and now return to you two more talents than you gave to me."
>
> The master replied to this servant the same as he did to the first servant. And the second servant joyously walked on down to the main house.
>
> Now, the third servant walked up to the master and with a sly grin on his face said to him, "Master, I know your reputation in the business community. You are a hard man to deal with. I was afraid of what might happen to me if I invested the talent you gave me and lost your money. So I buried it in the ground, and here it is."
>
> The master's face grew red with rage. "You lazy, good for nothing servant! If you were so afraid of me, you should have at least put the talent in the bank where it would have gotten minimal interest. Here," he grabbed the talent from the servant's hand, "give it to the servant with the ten talents. And listen to this lesson—the one who has will be given even more. The one with nothing? Even what little he has will be taken away!" (*author's paraphrase*)

Even though the parable was told with a more divine purpose in mind, and the spiritual lessons and references to the final judgment are obvious, the practical applications and lessons on economic development and money management skills are clear. **While we are to be good stewards of the gifts the Lord has given us, successful economic development and money management skills are the key to our being able to fulfill here on earth the work the Lord has left for us to do.**

How can we as African American Christians—who have been historically disenfranchised from full participation in the American economic system — ever hope to fully take part in this stewardship? Until very recently, with the proliferation of programs such as the federally mandated Empowerment Zones located in the midst of the most neglected areas of our urban centers, our major financial institutions did not see the economic advantage of investing money in our cities (even though African American churches deposit millions of dollars each week into their coffers).

Now the tide seems to be turning. Established banks are stumbling over one another trying to align themselves with projects that are being planned in the Empowerment Zones. More African American owned banks than ever before are being started by black investors and are making a difference in the amount of dollars being invested within our communities.

Given this surge of financial energy in our midst, what can we do to take advantage of the current wave of economic opportunity? The intent of this chapter is to show what the church and community must do to be good stewards in the area of economic development. The doors of opportunity are ready to swing open; they are just waiting for us to knock!

Think about It

In the space below, list ways in which:

- your church encourages its members to take part in the resurgence of interest in economic development in our cities
- your church has presented workshops and seminars that explain to the church membership and surrounding community the economic opportunities currently available to them
- your church has facilitated a dialogue between financial institutions and your congregation
- if your church has a credit union, it provides financial planning services and counseling to its depositors

____

____

____

____

____

____

____

____

____

____

List any new programs your church could start that would aid members and the community in taking advantage of the economic opportunities available to them.

____

____

____

____

____

____

____

____

____

____

Focus

In remarks given at the National African American Family Ministry Conference, Rev. Dr. Wallace Charles Smith, pastor of Shiloh Baptist Church of Washington, D.C., described the communal structure as the key to understanding African American economics as well as the basic structure of the black church. Smith elaborated, “We as a people are interconnected. That’s one of the chief strengths that we bring to the equation. The extended family notion [to be discussed later in this book] is a ticket to health and well-being if we can maximize its potential.”

Smith continued, “Some of us remember when there was not a homeless problem in the African American community because we had an informal system of adoption. When someone was down and out, they dropped in and stayed until they got themselves together and moved out.”

Interconnectedness, communalism, and adopting the underdog must carry over into our notions of financial empowerment if we are to make the most of our potential for economic strength. Mortgage and insurance red-lining, discrimination in processing loan applications, and unwritten but stringently enforced restrictive housing covenants are obstacles that have been deliberately built into the fiber of our society’s economy to keep out those who "do not belong." This makes it all the more mandatory that we seek united and collective means to combat and obliterate these formidable roadblocks to financial empowerment.

In addition, the social safety nets that were at one time provided by the government and that sustained whole families and sometimes entire communities with crippling effectiveness are being systematically and effectively demolished. The money is being channeled elsewhere. The checks are not coming in the mail. We have nowhere else to turn but to our own resources. Fortunately, these resources are plentiful and ready to be tapped. We must, however, put ourselves, both individually and collectively, in a position to use them.

Smith lists three key ingredients that must be developed in the African American community in order to maximize the potential strength of our economic development: communalism, cooperation, and stewardship.

As mentioned above, communalism is one of the enduring strengths of our African American heritage. The notion of extended family and interrelatedness must be included in any program that is expected to provide the type of economic effect that will lift a community crippled by fiscal neglect and institutional abuse out of its misery. We need strength, and that will develop only by pooling monetary resources as well as time, energy, and skills.

The church can provide the structure that brings all of this together:

- a building to house an economic training and development program;
- a meeting place for pastors committed to leading by example as they connect their individual visions for revitalized neighborhoods into one united front;
- congregations that are comprised of people who are willing to take the first step and receive training or even retraining in economic development skills and entrepreneurship.

An example of just such a pooling effort is described in the "Guideposts" section below.

The second key ingredient, cooperation, does not automatically flow from communalism. Yet it is so vital to the community that it is also known as *Ujamaa* (cooperative economics) and is one of the *Nguzo*

Saba — the seven values of Kwanzaa. Given its importance, we must also admit that a significant impediment to an effective cooperative effort must be overcome before the major players — our African American churches — can be the power brokers they were called to be in this field of economic revitalization and empowerment. Smith refers to the "intertribal rivalries" that manifest themselves as churches sometimes stake out their own territories, often in the same neighborhood. Competing for the same constituents and for the biggest share of the revitalization pie, these church rivalries can resemble — on a much smaller scale — some of the tribal rivalries that have taken place throughout history and that tragically still occur in nations around the world from Europe to the Middle East, Africa, Asia, and South America.

Realizing the power of a collective vision and shared goals, these divisive "rivalries" and arbitrarily determined boundaries can and should be set aside for the pursuit of the common good. But the pastors and the members of their congregations have to be willing to see past the comfortable confines of their own churches and acknowledge their role in helping to meet the needs of the broader society. They have to get comfortable with the give and take necessary for effective cooperation. The single voice must be willing to be merged into the common voice for the common good.

The third factor, stewardship, must also be embraced as a necessary component of economic development. Smith goes beyond the standard dictionary definition of stewardship as being the management of another's property, finances, or other affairs. Rather, he defines stewardship as the principle of accepting responsibility over the things God has entrusted into our care. *Responsibility* is the key term. When we accept responsibility for the well-being of one another and the good of the whole, we can approach economic development as a natural outgrowth of stewardship and as a part of our heritage of care from within the extended family.

The Word

The biblical concept of stewardship is presented in a variety of ways throughout the Scriptures. Matthew 14:17 describes the feeding of the five thousand with five loaves of bread and two fish. In this instance, stewardship becomes an example of trusting that the resources at hand will be sufficient to do the job that needs to be done. When Jesus was told what was available, he did not tell the disciples to go and not come back until they had gathered enough food to feed five thousand men plus women and children. He simply said, "Fine, bring the food here to me." Once he had the food in hand, he blessed it and then used it to get the job done. That is stewardship combined with faith and resourcefulness. Today, some two thousand years later, that same kind of stewardship can transform a meager donation to a small urban church into a business planning seminar for a room full of entrepreneurs. Or, as in the case of Greater Christ Baptist Church in Detroit, it can turn a row of burned-out storefronts into a thriving Burger King franchise.

Leviticus 25:10 portrays the jubilee year — the fiftieth year — as a time when each person returns to his own property. No work shall be done on the land during the jubilee year. Instead, it will be a holy year and a time when certain land that has been sold is reclaimed by the original owner. Those who purchase and own this land during the intervening years from jubilee to jubilee are merely *stewards* of the property. They are not to cheat one another. Instead, they are to follow certain prescribed rules of fairness: fairness for the buyer and seller and fairness in the sale and distribution of the crops from the land.

In addition, Leviticus 25:23–24 says that the land, when it is sold, will not be sold forever, for the land belongs to the Lord. Instead, in each transaction a provision will be made for the redemption of the land.

The purpose of these Leviticus passages is to assure that no one profits unfairly or for too long from property to which he has no permanent rights. Any transaction must be made with an eye toward the fact that one day the property will be returning to someone else. This is biblically mandated stewardship — fairness in caring for something else until it reverts to its original owner.

This type of fairness in stewardship is necessary to sustain successful economic development even today. Economic development — combined with notions of communality, cooperation, and stewardship — means that we are working toward a goal that will be shared with others in the community both now and in the future. Nothing belongs to us solely or permanently. We are merely caretakers of this society until it is time to hand the controls over to another generation in another time.

Matthew 20:1–16 describes an equitable use of power. Jesus, represented by the landowner, decides to pay the laborers who have worked only one hour the same wages as the laborers who have worked a full day. Amid grumbling from the full-day laborers, Jesus answers, "Is it not lawful for me to do what I will with mine own?" Can't I do what I want with my own money, and property, and business?

The lessons from this parable still hold true today: economic success does give us certain powers that we would not ordinarily have. The goal is to use them for the good of all and in a just way, as demonstrated by Jesus in the way he treats the two levels of laborers.

Guideposts

By the time readers reach this point in the chapter, they will want to know how they can facilitate the economic development of their own communities and the families in those communities. More specifically, they will want to examine the role of the church in facilitating such development. The model we will examine was developed by the Detroit Eastside Coalition of Churches founded by the author in Detroit.

The Detroit Eastside Coalition of Churches (DECC) was founded in 1993 as the ecumenical response of twenty pastors from the east side of Detroit to the crisis economic conditions facing the residents in their church areas. These clergy believe that the issues of crime, lack of decent and affordable housing, inadequate public transportation, and a decline in health care services are all rooted in the economic downturn that is keenly felt by the residents of Detroit. In addition, these pastors believe that the best way to address these issues is to attack the root problem — lack of economic opportunity — as a coalition and thereby help the residents to create their own economic opportunities.

After the formation of DECC, the organization immediately began the process of pursuing appropriate avenues of self-help for the residents of the DECC community. A survey conducted for one of the member churches by a state university indicated a high level of interest in the economic revitalization of the area. There was a desire for a return to an era of "self-help" economic progress.

The members of DECC immediately saw the potential of tapping this groundswell of support within the community by instituting an Entrepreneurial Development Center as a means to introduce the concepts of entrepreneurship and self-help to the residents of the DECC area. This venture provides a church-based institution for training and experience in various areas of business activity, which then acts as a springboard for future business development and self-help projects for the DECC constituency. The Entrepreneurial Development Center is comprised of a coalition of entities representing conventional lending institutions, the academic community, and the corporate community.

Because it represents a broad coalition of churches from within the community and presented a strategic plan ready for immediate implementation, DECC was awarded a major grant from a national foundation to facilitate the opening of the Entrepreneurial Development Center. The center offers a training program that introduces area residents to concepts of entrepreneurship and self-help that include business plan development, individual and group counseling, supplemental start-up loans, and referrals to additional resources throughout the city. The center tailors its services to meet the needs of individual clients, whose levels of skill and education range from GED diplomas to MBA degrees. The scope of the center also entails providing training and experience in various areas of business activity that can be a springboard for future business development and self-help projects for the DECC constituency. When the client/entrepreneur is ready, the center's business start-up program is able to provide the assistance and support necessary to help the entrepreneur.

A key element in the success of the center's business start-up program is the availability of a *micro-enterprise loan fund.* Combining the money available from the loan fund (generally in amounts ranging from $500 to $1,500 with repayment completed within one year from the date of the loan) with any money invested by the entrepreneur, the client's business venture is given a key financial boost. Timely repayment insures that funds are available for other entrepreneurs and also gives the new business a direct stake in the success of *other* new businesses in the community who are depending on the loan fund to help them with their own start-up business costs.

After recognizing the level of business training received by and entrepreneurial success enjoyed by Entrepreneurial Development Center clients, two major banks, who have made a commitment to be a part of the federally mandated Empowerment Zone, have agreed to accept referrals of center clients. These clients must have completed the training program, begun their business venture, successfully repaid their microenterprise loan, and become ready for an additional infusion of working capital to sustain or expand their business.

DECC and the Entrepreneurial Development Center are prime examples of the ability of diverse elements of the community to join together to work toward the economic revitalization of an area and the economic development of the resources available to the families in the area.

Q & A

Question: How did you get so many pastors to work together in forming the Detroit Eastside Coalition of Churches?

Answer: The needs of the community were so great—and still are—that whatever denominational, personality, or vision differences may have existed between the member pastors, the desire to help the community outweighed all of that. As we have discussed in great detail in this chapter, nothing can be accomplished alone; the extended family, communal outlook is essential to the success of any project with broad impact and long-range goals. DECC's member pastors know this and are willing and eager to work together to see that economic development takes root in their area.

Question: What can be done on a small scale if your area doesn't have a coalition of pastors who want to work together or you cannot get major funding for your project?

Answer: Plenty! Start with seminars in your church for your congregation and the surrounding community. Be attentive to the topics that are of interest to your church members and community residents and invite speakers to the church to address those topics. Even an occasional seminar can provide valuable information and inspiration to those who are eager to work toward a long-range goal of economic development.

Small has a way of growing. What may look like a puny start now, with groundswell support, can become a major program with interest from different segments of the community. The important thing is to get started. Growth will come if church members and the community feel that their needs have been considered in the plans you have made.

Highlights

Listed below are some of the crucial aspects to consider when planning economic development projects in a community. At the end of this list, add other points that are important to your understanding of this topic.

- We must seek united and collective means to combat and obliterate roadblocks to economic empowerment.
- Three key ingredients necessary to maximize the potential strength of our economic development plans are communalism, cooperation, and stewardship.
- The notion of extended family and interrelatedness must be included in any program that is expected to provide an economic lift to the community.
- The model of the Detroit Eastside Coalition of Churches is one of a church-based institution that trains clients in various aspects of business activity and that acts as a springboard for future business development and self-help projects.
-
-
-
-
-

Think about It – Again

Think about the information that has been presented in this chapter. Now consider again what new programs and ministries could be implemented by your church to encourage economic development in your community.

____

____

____

____

____

____

____

____

____

____

CHAPTER FIVE

Creating Healthy Communities

Up Front

The mandate to our churches can be stated plainly: *The church has a responsibility for the temporal as well as the spiritual redemption of the community it inhabits.*

Following that mandate, it is easy enough for pastors and elders to look around, point their finger at evidences of decay, crime, lawlessness, and abandonment, and shake their heads. They can see what needs to be done; that is the simple part. But once they recognize the need, what are the churches to do?

Often churches are the last viable entities remaining in their communities. They stay in some neighborhoods long after almost every other legitimate structure has left. The grocery stores, dry cleaners, and barber shops move. Local public schools close because of a decrease in enrollment. More prosperous residents move to other, more desirable, parts of the city and the suburbs. But the churches stick it out. Even if the only reason the churches remain is because it would cost too much to construct or purchase a new building elsewhere, their presence says something to the surrounding community—namely, that there is at least one entity of worth that has not left. There is at least one entity that does not mind remaining in the midst of what these residents cannot or choose not to leave. *There is hope.* And being a standard of hope for a community is an excellent place to start when you want to make an impact in their midst.

So if the church has a visible presence and it has created goodwill with the residents just by remaining, the next step is very simple: take a stand on something. Make a public statement by the outreach ministries the church promotes throughout the community. Make a public statement by organizing a community forum on a selected topic and holding the forum in the church sanctuary or fellowship hall. Make the stand something visible, worthwhile, and life-changing to the community.

If drug addiction is a problem, form a partnership with a local hospital or with a professional counselor who attends the church and open up a substance abuse counseling center in the church. If there is a high dropout rate among the teens in the community, open in the church Sunday school rooms an adult education center where teens can earn a GED. If many of the single mothers have been removed from the welfare roles, open a day care center while providing a job training referral service to these mothers.

The list of options that would make a dramatic impact on the quality of life in the community is almost endless. It is exciting to even begin to consider and list the wonderful possibilities. But the church has to start with one of them. It is not enough to look at another church and say, "Well, they have more educated members, or their neighborhood has not deteriorated to the extent of ours." There are no excuses. The time is now.

This chapter will examine some of the ways a church can make a dramatically positive impact on the community it inhabits. With vision, tenacity, and creativity, the prescriptions given by one church can be followed by any church. The church institution that has survived for two thousand years—even in the midst of horrible persecution—can surely muster up these qualities.

Read this chapter and see what can be done, and then decide, "What am *I* going to do?"

Think about It

In the space below, consider the area where your church is located, what viable structures remain, and what social problems are the most pressing. Then determine:

- how your church has responded to any of the most urgent social problems witnessed in the neighborhood

- how your church has made its presence felt among the community residents
- why your congregation has decided to stay in its present location

____

____

____

____

____

____

____

____

____

List below any new programs that could be initiated by your church that would help to restore health to the surrounding community.

____

____

____

____

____

____

____

____

____

Focus

The church must take two essential steps in order to begin a ministry or series of ministries that work to create healthy communities. These steps have been analyzed by Rev. Nicholas Hood III, pastor of Plymouth United Church of Christ in Detroit. Hood was a presenter at the National African American Family Ministry Conference.

First, the church must assess the state of the community, determining the obvious needs of the people who still live in the area. These may include:

affordable single-family and multifamily housing

better street lighting

crime prevention

recreational activities

environmental cleanup

jobs and retraining opportunities

quality retail opportunities

The list may appear intimidating, but the church only has to choose to accomplish one thing at a time.

"However," cautions Hood, "one of the biggest mistakes the church can make is to start building something without having taken the time to consider the true needs of the community." The true needs of the community can be discovered by seeking input from residents who have remained when others have left. No matter what the church may want to build or rebuild, if the neighborhood does not want it — if the key residents do not see a need for it — they will not support it, use it, or refer others to it once it is built. Then what good has been done for the community and its residents? The church's actions cannot create healthy communities if the agent for change is perceived as something less than desirable.

After assessing the needs and seeking input from residents, the church must decide on a positive solution for the chosen problem. That can sometimes be the most daunting aspect of the initial project stages. Suppose your church opts for a health clinic. Where do you start? According to Hood, "The church should always start by lobbying the appropriate governmental agencies for the sources of solutions. Our local governments owe certain services to its citizens for the tax dollars they receive."

If the government agency balks, the church should remember the tremendous power it wields in the form of having a congregation of registered voters and remind the government agency of that fact. The government is there to assist *you!*

In the example of a health clinic, the government agency can help the church access certain block grant funds available from the federal government to be used in rebuilding particular types of core city neighborhoods. The agency may also facilitate introductions between a major health provider and the church. The church can then use its power to insist on certain benefits from the health care provider such as increased or guaranteed privileges for African American doctors to work at the clinic. If the immunization schedules are not being met by a large percentage of inner-city residents, the church can ask the health provider to mount an intensive campaign from within the community to see that all children under the age of three are immunized. Concerned with the high rate of prostate cancer among African American males, the church can ask for a mobile screening unit to travel into the community to conduct blood tests that can detect the earliest stages of this disease.

In pursuing the health clinic example, the church will have gone from a "What can we do?" stage to a "Look at all that we have been able to accomplish!" stage. The community will have acquired a state of the art health clinic in its midst. Provisions will have been made so that the physicians working the clinic reflect the ethnic makeup of the community. And positive inroads will have been initiated regarding black mortality rates as they affect infants and African American males. Health — both literally and figuratively — can be restored to the community as a result of the church's vision and the proper use of its God-given powers.

The Word

The Bible emphatically affirms the church's ministry of community healing. Hood looks to several New Testament verses as a basis for that affirmation. First, in Matthew 16:18 Jesus says to Peter, "Upon this rock I will build my church; and the gates of hell shall not prevail against it." This statement of the power of the church translates itself to all aspects of the church's work within the community. Nothing shall keep the work of the church from going forward. No obstacles will prevent the vision of the church from being ultimately realized. The Lord has given the church a position of power that we are encouraged to rely upon as we make the church the cornerstone of our ministries.

James 5:14 concerns the church and healing. "Is any sick among you?

let him call for the elders of the church; and let them pray over him." Is *any* sick among you? That includes individuals, communities, families—the church is there as an instrument of healing.

In Ephesians 1:22–23 we see that Jesus Christ is the ultimate source of the church's power. "[God] hath put all things under [Christ's] feet, and gave him to be the head over all things to the church, which is his body, the fulness of him that filleth all in all." Is the church to break through walls of bureaucracy in appealing to the government for certain sources of funding or referrals to different agency department heads? The source of that power is Christ. Is the church to garner support from apathetic or suspicious community residents? The source of that power is Christ. Is the church to have the faith to embark upon an ambitious community revitalization project when everyone else has abandoned the area? The source of that power is Christ. The mission of the church requires such an extraordinary vision beyond what is commonplace and acceptable that only the supernatural power of Christ can give the church the power to both envision and accomplish the task.

Finally, Acts 2:44–47 describes the sharing of resources between the believers of the early church. That is the model to be copied by all Christians. "And all that believed were together, and had all things common; and sold their possessions and goods, and parted them to all men, as every man had need." The church, as it works to realize its ministry of healing within the community, is a strong example of the sharing of resources. Using whatever resources it has for the benefit of the entire community exemplifies the Christian model of caring for the needs of others. By pooling the resources of the group, we can accomplish a level of success that individual initiative usually cannot achieve.

Guideposts

Hood's church has a long history of community redevelopment. In the summer of 1967, Plymouth Church dedicated 220 units of low- to moderate-income housing in an area of Detroit that was formerly called Black Bottom. The road to that moment began several years earlier in 1960 when the church leadership discovered that the city had voted to tear down everything in that area except for the Catholic churches. The plan was to use that part of the city as a major medical center.

Hood says, "The church looked at different areas where they could possibly move. They prayed as a body and came to the decision that God had called them to that area and not only were they going to stay in that section of the city but they were going to *rebuild* the area." That was the only way they could assure the residents in the community that there would continue to be housing — affordable housing — available for them.

So in 1963 Hood's church formed a housing corporation. This was a visionary move, because in 1963 the law did not even allow for the nonprofit development of housing. But because of that visionary act, by 1967 the church was able to access a recently created federal program known as 231 D-3, and the church was awarded a grant of $3 million.

In 1972 Hood's church built and relocated to a new church building only one block away from where the original structure had stood. Also in 1972 the church wanted to develop another parcel of land. However, by this time the rules had changed. The federal government had started what is known as the "limited dividend partnership program." In order to comply with the guidelines of this program, Hood's church needed a major partner with a large amount of money to invest. They were able to link up with the Chrysler Corporation (now known as Daimler Chrysler). Says Hood, "Chrysler became a general partner and put together a group of limited partners. The partners got a very attractive tax write off of 90 percent of the whole project costs after putting up 10 percent of those costs. The government supplied the rest of the funding."

That setup worked so well that Hood's church arranged another development project in the same way. In the first instance, the church formed a nonprofit corporation that is a co-owner in the project. In the second development project, the church is not a co-owner because they did not invest any of their own money into it.

In 1972 Hood's church also created what has become a $2 million per year corporation known as the Cyprian Center. Hood explains, "The center assists mentally handicapped persons with capacities ranging from the very lowest functioning levels to actually very high functioning levels. The first unit built was a day activity center that serves one hundred people per day. Then there are the residential units that house small groups of mentally handicapped people: two are on site and the rest are located across the city."

More recently the church's elementary school was classified as a charter school. They are in discussions with a major university to develop a partnership with the university's charter middle school. Another future project the church is interested in developing is a high quality assisted living senior complex.

Hood's church does not make any profit on any of these projects. That was never their goal. However, by positioning itself to pursue all possible channels of help and partnership as they become available, the church has done a remarkable job of breathing life and health back into an area that had been written off as expendable by the city planners.

Q & A

Question: These programs sound wonderful, but our church seems to be stuck in a rut. How can we catch hold of a vision for the community?

Answer: Look at the real needs of your community. Talk to members of your church who live in the community. Go out into the neighborhoods and talk to the people who may never have even set foot inside your church. Shop where they shop. Stand at the bus stops. Get to know the life of the area. The needs will come jumping out at you.

Then align your church with the expertise necessary to formulate a vision plan. There is help — free of charge — at local, state, and national levels. Contact your city or state housing, education, or nonprofit development authority and ask to be referred to a technical assistance provider. Contact a local hospital or health care provider to arrange to talk to someone in their community outreach area. The wealth of information and assistance available just for the asking is almost staggering.

Question: Doesn't all of this emphasis on community health and redevelopment take our eyes off the real mission of the church — to spread the gospel of Jesus Christ?

Answer: Rev. Hood answers, "The church has a responsibility to not only lead its parishioners to the throne of grace through prayer, preaching, and singing, but also through our mission to rebuild our communities in the spirit of Jesus Christ. I consider Jesus and all that he did for society: I find it interesting that he tended to associate himself with the poor, the dispossessed, and the downtrodden of the earth. I am confident that if Christ were alive today, he would not focus simply on the saving of souls but on the quality of the lives of those souls. Jesus said, 'I come that you might have life and that you might have it more abundantly' " (John 10:10, *his paraphrase*).

Highlights

Listed below are some of the principal points discussed in this chapter on creating healthy communities. At the end of this list, add other items that are important to establishing the needs of the community and facilitating the road back to health.

- The church has a responsibility for the temporal as well as the spiritual redemption of the community it serves.
- The church must determine the needs of the community.
- The church must decide on a positive solution for these problems.
- The Bible affirms the church's ministry of community healing.
- The goal of the church is to position itself to pursue all available channels of help and partnership as they become available.
-
-
-
-
-

Think about It – Again

In light of the information presented in this chapter, think again about what ministries and programs your church could implement to create revitalized and healthy communities.

CHAPTER SIX

Nurturing Marriage

Up Front

"And the LORD God formed man of the dust of the ground, and breathed into his nostrils the breath of life; and man became a living soul. . . . And the LORD God took man, and put him into the garden of Eden to dress it and to keep it. . . . And out of the ground the LORD God formed every beast of the field, and every fowl of the air; and brought them unto Adam to see what he would call them: and whatsoever Adam called every living creature, that was the name thereof. . . . And the LORD God caused a deep sleep to fall upon Adam, and he slept: and he took one of his ribs. . . . And the rib, which the LORD God had taken from man, made he a woman, and brought her unto the man." (Genesis 2:7,15,19,21–22)

The Lord created man and woman to keep and cultivate this special place — the garden of Eden. The work that the Lord gave them was meant to be enjoyable. Looking at Genesis 2:15, we see that God put Adam in the garden to nurture it and look after it. It was the lushest and most perfect place on the earth, and all Adam had to do was take care of it. Can you imagine being asked to care for something that was already perfect and was meant to remain perfect? It was work, but it was also pleasure.

Even naming the animals was a joy. God brought them before Adam, and whatever name Adam chose, that was the animal's name. Antelope, lion, canary, lamb, goat, squirrel, donkey — Adam called the animals as he saw fit, and the Lord approved of all that he did. Even the woman the Lord made from Adam to be his helper was given no restrictions. The man and woman were one flesh, a perfect union. They were meant to be together and to work together in this perfect garden.

Then came trouble. Enmity came into the garden, and the man and woman engaged in lying, betrayal, and deceit. They would no longer know the same level of perfect intimacy. For the man, cultivating the soil would be hard toil. For the woman, the union with her husband would be rewarded with pain in childbirth. The lush garden would be only a memory, because they were banished from it forever.

Today the institution of marriage — the union between a man and a woman — is still suffering from the effects of this banishment. Men and women try to make their marriages work, but too often they have no feeling of joy as they work to maintain their union. Instead of looking forward to joyfully cultivating a lush garden, couples enter a marriage expecting to find, once the honeymoon is over, the hard toil of cultivating rocky soil.

Will there ever be a way to erase the enmity between men and women that has infected the institution of marriage? Will couples ever reclaim the joy that is inherent in pursuing a lifelong commitment to each other? Will the door to the garden ever be opened again?

The emphatic answer is yes, we can get back to the garden! Cultivating our marriages can be a joyful experience. Husbands and wives helping one another in a common task and with a shared vision can be a reality. And the church has a vital role in helping couples to achieve these things. By putting Christ — the Redeemer — at the head of the church, God made a dramatic statement: the church is a necessary tool in the redemption process that will lead us back to paradise and the joy of the garden of Eden. The church will play a pivotal part in healing the wounds that fester in marriages and that keep husbands and wives from knowing the full measure of the joy waiting before them.

This chapter will examine the needs of marriages in the twenty-first century. It will also highlight specific support that the church can offer to couples as they seek to strengthen and enhance their marriages. When the church — already empowered by God — begins to tap the reserves of that power, the results can be nothing less spectacular than pointing us back in the direction of the garden of Eden.

Think about It

Take a few minutes to write in the space provided below some ways in which:

- your church has developed ministries and programs to strengthen and revitalize marriages
- your church supports couples in their attempts to maintain Christ-centered marriages
- your church has carefully examined the specific needs of the couples in the church and community and tailored its ministries to meet those particular needs

Considering the specific needs of the families in your church and the surrounding community, list below any new programs and ministries that could be implemented by your church to help marriages flourish.

Focus

The African roots of creation are clear from the beginning of the Word. In the Genesis 2:13 naming of the rivers that flow from the garden of Eden, the second river — Gihon — is described as surrounding the land of Cush. This clearly establishes the connection between Cush, the ancient name of the kingdom of Ethiopia, and the creation garden.

Given the special relationship between Africa, the Bible, and the origins of man and woman, it is only natural to suggest that African American Christians look to African models of family and relationship as a means to strengthen the bonds between couples in marriages.

These African models of family are based on notions of "communal" care in the family structure and a sense of "connectivity" between these same family members. In actual situations this means that no one is left to fend for themselves. One person's pain is shared by all. The progress of a family — or even the well-being of all of the families in an entire village — is dependent on uplifting the potential of all to succeed. In a marriage this means joining two lives into one. Marriage partners must consider themselves to be inseparably connected to each other. What affects one affects the other. When one hurts, the other feels the pain. When one rejoices, the other cries tears of joy. The marriage prospers because both the man and woman are committed to seeing that their spouse is prospering physically, emotionally, and spiritually. To the best of their ability, they care for each other as they care for themselves.

Of course, this sounds ideal. Anyone would want a marriage relationship based on these principles. Problems arise, however, when couples are actually immersed in the throes of a financial crisis, when communication issues make it difficult to understand each other's roles in the marriage, when one or the other has been laid off from a job, or when a much wanted pregnancy ends in miscarriage. These crises can tear apart even the strongest of relationships. How can communal notions of care be called upon when the pain is personal and is hitting hard upon the individual? In such times it is hard to think about sharing pain when the first thought to cross our minds is, "This is so terrible, who could possibly want to bear this with me?" Or even, "How could they have the nerve to think they know what I'm feeling — I'm the one who lost the baby (or got fired from the job or ran up charges on the credit cards, etc.)."

When we hurt, we quite often just want to lick our wounds, go off into a corner, and be left alone.

What is the answer? We have to turn to the Bible and to the creation of man and woman. When Eve was created, God called her a "help meet," — that is, someone who *helps* the spouse *meet* the challenges as well as the joys of their life together. A marriage relationship cannot achieve help-meet status just by willing it to be so: the man and woman must be compatible — that is, they must agree to conduct themselves and their marriage in such a way that they will come together and serve, encourage, share, assist, labor, relieve, and comfort. Obviously, the list is even longer and can be completed by each couple as they assess the needs and goals of their marriage. But the important point is that the couple agrees to this joint goal.

This agreement to realize help-meet status can be more easily obtained if the partners in the marriage strive to maintain compatibility in three crucial areas:

1. *Physical:* the husband and wife kindle and rekindle their physical attraction for one another.

2. *Intellectual:* the husband and wife seek to know one another in order to appreciate and nurture the uniqueness of their partner's personality.

3. *Spiritual/emotional:* the husband and wife both welcome the presence of God in their marriage.

It is in maintaining and even striving for compatibility in these three areas that many, if not most, marriages need the greatest amount of help. It is the duty of the church — a vital instrument of healing in the redemption process — to provide this support to couples as they seek to become helpers to one another and united as one before God.

The Word

The Bible contains explicit images and specific directions for building and maintaining the marital connection. Genesis 2:25 describes, in one sentence, the perfection of the union between Adam and Eve and their relationship with God. In the beginning God was the head of the union between Adam and Eve, and their relationship with God and with each other was built on trust. They were naked, but they were not ashamed. Nakedness had no meaning to them because they had nothing to hide from each other. More importantly, they had nothing to hide from God. Adam and Eve looked at each other and saw perfection. They trusted each other. They listened to God's voice and heard the counsel of the Father of the universe. They trusted God. They had no wants other than what was provided for them in the garden; their desire was pure. God was at the head of their relationship because, since the time of their creation, they had known no other way to maintain their union with each other and with their Creator.

Yet when Adam accepted the invitation of Eve to taste of the fruit of the tree of the knowledge of good and evil, he put the woman above God. Adam listened to Eve's counsel and ignored God's commandment. The sacred foundation of trust that united the man and woman under God by a bond of trust was broken. The relationship was in trouble; Adam and Eve were then driven — by their own sin — to hide from their Creator.

As heart-wrenching and cataclysmic as the original breach of trust was to the order of the garden and future of all humanity, a lack of trust in a marriage today is still devastating to a husband and wife. When one or both of the partners hides from the other and from God — either physically or emotionally — because they have listened to a voice other than the voice of God, the relationship has lost its unity. The bond of trust needs to be recaptured, and that is no easy task. Adam and Eve were banished from the garden of Eden when they broke the bond of their sacred trust with God. It took the blood of Jesus, the Holy Redeemer, to open the way for a return to the garden. It still takes the blood of Jesus to point the way for a man and a woman to reclaim the trust that has been lost in their marriage because trust is the foundation of marriage. The only way trust can be restored is by putting God back at the head of the marriage, listening to his counsel, and then standing on that word.

The process is difficult because at first the couple will feel the shame of their nakedness and, as did Adam and Eve, try to hide from God. But with time — and that can mean days or possibly years — the cleansing blood of Jesus will allow them to understand that they have nothing to hide. By acknowledging the headship of God, the husband and wife can work to reclaim the foundation of trust that will reunite them as one in their marriage.

Guideposts

The role of the church as a vehicle for encouraging and maintaining trust and compatibility in marriages is the cornerstone of its ministry to the family. It is the duty of the church to make opportunities for couples to come together and learn how to build or maintain unity and a foundation of trust in their marriage. Four essential channels through which the church can provide this service to couples are:

- prayer sessions
- counseling
- mentoring/testimonies
- classes on marriage related issues

Prayer sessions for married couples — both individually and as a group — are an essential tool for couples to either keep or invite God into a headship position in the marriage. Group prayer sessions can occur weekly or monthly, whichever the pastor gauges as necessary based on his knowledge of the needs of the congregation. This is also an excellent way for couples to enjoy Christian fellowship and support from like-minded couples. Husbands and wives receive encouragement from these group prayer sessions to maintain prayer time in the home. Joining in prayer either daily or weekly, they can never seek the counsel of God too much or too often as they work to maintain that crucial bond of trust.

Counseling services offered to these married couples differ from those offered to couples who are in a divorce prevention mode (see chapter 8). In seeking to build trust or maintain the headship of God in their marriage, the counseling sessions for these couples are geared toward strengthening interpersonal/compatibility skills, such as communication, goal setting, parenting, and other relationship enhancement abilities. Greater Christ Baptist Church in Detroit (one of the organizing churches for the National African American Family Ministry Conference) offers workshops, seminars, and retreats to its married couples through its Living Skills Institute. Social workers, psychologists, and various mental health professionals from within both the church and community present carefully designed sessions that address issues that work to impede the progress of couples in developing trusting relationships.

Working closely with the pastor and eliciting input from husbands and wives in the congregation, the workshop presenters offer practical guidance that is custom designed to meet the needs of the congregation. A workshop agenda would include:

- open discussion time
- a presentation by the speaker
- a question and answer session
- presentation of additional material by the speaker
- a second question and answer session
- wrap-up remarks
- a closing time of prayer

The goal of such a workshop or seminar is to always place at the couples' disposal useful techniques that they can take from the gathering and put into practice in their homes and marriages. Also, being in regular contact with other married couples who hold similar visions for their marriages and who are struggling with the same sorts of issues offers invaluable moments of fellowship and peer support.

It is important that couples never feel that they are struggling alone or that their goals are unattainable. One method of making this assurance is through group mentoring programs. These mentoring programs are different from those offered to boys and girls who need exposure to additional male and female role models. At Greater Christ Baptist Church the entire church is a witness to married couples who are singled out as an encouragement for everyone in congregation.

The "50 and Counting Club" recognizes couples in the church who have been married for fifty or more years. These couples serve as models of commitment for the whole church. They are recognized during a church service and at special events throughout the year. Often their testimonies are featured in the church newsmagazine. This is the church's way of recognizing and encouraging God's plan for a lifelong marital commitment; it also shows everyone — children, teens, single adults, and married couples — the living fruit of a trusting relationship that holds God at its head.

The Annual Family Day at Greater Christ Baptist Church emphasizes the importance of family life and honors the Family of the Year. Although the Family of the Year may be a single adult who is devoted to the children's mentoring program or a grandparent who is raising an orphaned child, more often than not, the Family of the Year is a married couple who exhibits devotion to each other and to God. The couple is honored at the Family Day worship service and becomes one of the role models whose testimony can be emulated by others in the congregation.

Throughout the year, in the church newsmagazine and newsletter, couples are highlighted whose testimonies provide encouragement to the congregation and the community. Also, wedding anniversaries are celebrated. The goal of these programs is to provide living, vital encouragement to married couples, assuring them that they are not alone and that examples of Christ-centered marriages based on trust abound.

Q & A

Question: In helping spouses become help meets to one another, what if one spouse just will not budge in that direction? How does the remaining spouse go it alone?

Answer: That is a good and valid question. First Peter 3:1–2 describes how an ungodly spouse can be won over by observing the behavior of the believing spouse. Even if both spouses profess to be Christians, one spouse can still follow the prescription of Peter and set the example and tone of "helper" for the other to follow. Of course, the unwilling spouse may not budge for quite some time; it may be a circumstance that must be endured for years. However, the important role of the willing spouse is to be steadfast, confident that the marriage will one day attain the status ordained by God.

Question: Most of the couples in my congregation are busy with careers, family obligations, and hopefully other church commitments. How can I make an activity such as the married couples prayer sessions seem important enough that they will fit the time into their schedules to attend?

Answer: Your personal relationship with each couple will tell you which are most in need of these prayer times. Talk to these couples first. Impress upon them the importance of prayer in their individual and married lives. Once a core group of these couples begins to attend, others will see and follow their example.

Believe in the power of prayer! A change in the quality of their relationship will give even the most reluctant couples cause to keep returning while spreading the word about the value of these sessions to other couples.

Highlights

Below are some of the principal elements discussed in this chapter on building a marital relationship under God that is based on trust. Add at the end of this list other points that are essential to enhancing your church's ministry to married couples.

- The church must play a vital role in leading the institution of marriage back toward paradise.
- Marriage partners must consider themselves to be inseparably connected to each other.
- The husband and wife must conduct themselves in such a way that they will come together to serve, encourage, share, assist, labor, relieve, and comfort.
- Married couples must seek to maintain compatibility in three crucial areas: physical, intellectual, and spiritual/emotional.
- The Bible contains specific directions for building and maintaining the marital connection.

- Trust is the foundation of any marriage.
- The role of the church as a vehicle for encouraging and maintaining trust in marriages is the cornerstone of its ministry to the family.
-
-
-
-
-

Think about It – Again

In light of what has been presented in this chapter, consider again what new programs and ministries your church could implement to strengthen and enhance marriages in the congregation.

____

____

____

____

____

____

____

____

____

____

CHAPTER SEVEN

Parent-Teen Relationships

Up Front

Parenting has to be one of the most rewarding — yet challenging — experiences of our lives. The anticipation through nine months of pregnancy that culminates in the birth of a new life is a thrill that cannot be matched. We delight in watching our children grow and develop from rolling over, to crawling, to taking those first few wobbly steps, to actually running. We share in the joy of their accomplishments as they establish the skills, talents, and interests that are unique to them. As we watch them grow, we try to instill within them the values and conscience-building knowledge that will hold them on the right course as they become adults and make a life for themselves and their families.

But something happens between the joys of sharing their childhood and the pride of seeing the adults they have become: a stranger enters the house. The appearance of this stranger, though expected, is always a surprise. This stranger is commonly known as a *preteen* or *teenager.* At that point, our world — and their world — is not the same.

Where once a child would come home and chatter with a parent endlessly about school and friends, he or she now enters the kitchen with a grunt and answers all questions with the reply, "I don't know." Where a daughter might have sought her father's input on various matters, now when he tries to give his opinion she might snap back, "Daddy, you're old fashioned; you don't know what you're talking about!" Suddenly casual discussions about hair length, hair color, nail color, earrings in the nose, and five earrings on each ear quickly escalate from conversational tones to shouting matches.

The preteen and teen years are difficult for child and parent alike. It is new territory for both. Yet these years can be as exciting and rewarding as those early childhood years if we carry the right perspective and seek the right Wisdom. Having teenagers can be exhilarating for parents as we enter, or at least approach, a new period in our lives: middle age. As we will read below, many physiological and psychological changes are happening in us at the same time similar changes are occurring in our teenagers. We have common ground even in this turbulent developmental time!

Having teenagers is exciting because they want to try out for themselves so many of the lessons we taught them when they were little. They want to do for themselves so much of what they watched us do for them when they were younger. The Bible contains examples of teenagers stepping up to the challenge and showing that they were ready to cross the threshold to adulthood:

- Jesus was twelve years old when his parents found him in the temple amazing the rabbis with his understanding and wisdom.
- David was a teenager when he did what grown male soldiers could not do: he slew the giant Goliath.
- Daniel was a teenager when he was summoned into the service of King Nebuchadnezzar of Babylon. At that age the Lord gave him special wisdom and the gift of understanding visions and dreams.

And still today teenagers are stepping up to the challenge and showing a glimpse of the mighty men and women they will be as adults.

Dr. Phyllis J. Mayo, a clinical psychologist with a practice in Washington, D.C. — and one of the workshop presenters at the National African American Family Ministry Conference — provides valuable insight into the teen years and how we can best respond to and enjoy them. Her comments help us to get to know these "strangers in the house" and to welcome teens as much loved members of the family.

Think about It

Write on the lines below ways in which:

- you want to better understand your teenager
- you have been caught off guard by something your teenager has said or done
- you have been surprised by the level of maturity your teen has displayed in a certain situation
- you have been exasperated by the level of immaturity your teen has displayed in a certain situation

Now list ways in which you could improve your relationship with your teenager.

Focus

Raising a teenager is the only point in our cycle as parents when the changes in our lives correspond to the changes in the lives of our children. How do we handle the transitions of middle age and adolescence simultaneously? Often we cannot do an adequate job of it. That is when we must recognize that there is a problem and seek help from other sources. However, a new problem emerges among African American parents who would like to seek help — but do not — because of the negative cultural stigma attached to seeking the very help we need.

Dr. Mayo encourages parents of teenagers to admit that we do not have all of the answers and all of the skills and to call upon the services of ministers and counselors. Doing so will also encourage our teens to recognize that there are other people they can talk to who might help them through a difficult period in their development.

Helping us to understand what is behind, beneath, and around the turmoil of these stages, Mayo describes the similarities between adolescence and middle age. Looking at these similarities will help us to understand why teens and their parents can have a difficult time coping with and understanding one another.

Some of the obvious changes occurring with our teenagers are physical — growth spurts, hair growth in new places, body size and shape changes, and sexual development. Parents, on the other hand, experience weight gains and shifts, graying hair, and hair loss. Couples are concerned about the continuation of their marriage, and there is often a decrease in sexual activity.

Both parents and teens begin to question the value and role of religion in their lives. They are concerned about careers and employment — teens because they are close to the age of having to make a career decision, parents because they question the career decisions they made as teens and young adults.

Teenagers are starting to experiment with desires for independence yet still seek dependence. Parents, already independent, now feel the pull of dependence from elderly or ill parents.

Psychologically, teens are asking, "Who am I?" Parents are asking, "Who have I become, and is this how I want to be for the rest of my life?" Both teens and their parents are concerned with interpersonal relationships. Teens feel an urgency to fit into a group. Parents express that same urgency through career networking, overparticipation in church ministries, and active social calendars.

Though similar transitions are occurring, the teens are still children to their parents. Thus, it is up to the parents to provide the emotional stability and understanding necessary for their adolescents to achieve productive adulthood.

That is why counseling — outside help — can be so crucial at this stage in the family evolution. Families who can seek and use counseling services will find the enjoyment of maturity — both of the adolescent and of the parent who is approaching middle age — more easily within their grasp.

The Word

Mayo focuses on two Scriptures that are essential to effective parent-teen relationships. James 1:5 tells us, "If any of you lack wisdom, let him ask of God, that giveth to all men liberally." In the midst of so much turmoil that can be found in a household with one or more teenagers, it is crucial that parents remember to seek the Lord's wisdom. Instead of just reacting to situations as they occur with the adolescent, it is important that parents seek wisdom through prayer as well as in discussions with spiritual counselors.

In addition, it is important for teens to realize that this wisdom is from God and from their parents' own personal experiences. Parents should explain to their adolescents that certain decisions are made as the direct result of much prayer and discernment. This takes the decision-making process to a higher level and offers teens a working example of living the counsel of God.

The second passage is Ephesians 4:26: "Be ye angry and sin not: let not the sun go down upon your wrath." This is serious advice for a time period when tempers are flaring at a much higher rate than at other times in the parent-child relationship. With hormones raging and peer pressure at its greatest, the teen is more sensitive to rebuke and perceived slights than ever before.

Parents must be certain that any discipline of the teenager is not done in the heat of anger. The teen must not be subjected to physical or verbal abuse from punishment meted out in the heat of the moment. Teens should also be able to model their parents' example of restraint in learning to control their flare-ups of temper and anger.

Parents should seek and be ready to share with their teens other Scripture passages that offer guidance in their particular situation. Teenagers should be aware that their parents are actively seeking to understand what they are going through and are looking for ways to make their relationship the best that it can be.

Guideposts

In this section Mayo offers comments on topics important for maintaining smoothly functioning relationships between parents and teenagers.

- Communication is vital between parents and adolescents. If we turn a deaf ear to them, they will go to others who will listen, and these may be people we do not want them to be with. Often when teens are negatively influenced by peers it is because they are the only ones the teens feel will listen to what they have to say.

- What our teens say to us is important, even if it seems minor. We must listen to everything they have to say.

- Teens are sensitive; they need us. Even if they are pushing us away with their body language, they are waiting for us to come up and hug them.

- The most important time for the mother to be home for her child may not be when that child is an infant, but rather when he or she enters middle school. The transitions that occur at that time are more crucial and need the direct intervention of the parent (mother) more than at any other time. It is no accident that teen pregnancies often occur at home in the afternoon when the teen is home from school and the parent has not yet returned from work.

- Raising teens requires us to demonstrate how flexible we can be.
- We need to find out as much about what is going on in our teens' lives as possible. Snoop if you must. Be available to chauffeur to events and go on field trips. Parents have a responsibility to know what their teens are going through and who is influencing them.
- We must decide what our availability level is going to be for our teens and then schedule everything else around that.
- Remind teenagers that their experience level is low. A twelve-year-old should understand that his or her desire to take part in unsupervised personal relationships is unthinkable.
- Do not insist our teens do things our way. Give them guidance but let them understand that they have to learn to fight their own battles.
- Our expectations for our teens may lead them to depend on someone other than God. Instead, our actions and expectations should always lead them to depend on God.

Q & A

Question: How can I communicate with my teenager when I can't always understand my teenager's language?

Answer: That is a good question. We can only understand our teenagers' language if we spend time with them, talk with them, and ask them about what we cannot understand. If their language is too far removed from reality, it can mean that they are bonding too deeply with the peer group that speaks that language, which is to the detriment of their relationships with others. Parents need to help their teenagers communicate outside of that peer group by planning and including the teen in more family activities and outings.

Question: If my middle-age changes are occurring at the same time as my teenager's adolescent changes, who is looking after my needs?

Answer: The needs of your teenager come first. It is your responsibility as a parent to be there for your child. Seek counseling if necessary to understand the changes occurring in your own life, but know that your primary duty is to raise your children so that they can contribute to society as productive adults.

Highlights

Below are some of the main elements of effective parent-teen relationships. At the end of this list, add other crucial elements of effective parent-teen relationships.

- The teen years are the only time when changes in parents' lives correspond to changes in their teenagers' lives.
- Seek the services of a minister or counselor to help both parties in the parent-teen relationship.
- Though parents and teens are experiencing similar transitions, teens are still children.
- It is up to the parents to provide the emotional support and understanding necessary for their adolescent children.
- Listen to your teens.
- Be available to your teens.
- Our actions and expectations should always lead our teens to God.
-
-
-
-
-

Think about It – Again

Considering what you have read in this chapter, write in the space below how you can improve your relationship with your teenager.

____

____

____

____

____

____

____

____

____

____

CHAPTER EIGHT

Divorce: Preventive Measures

Up Front

In earlier generations marriages were arranged by the parents of young adults or teenagers. As old fashioned and restrictive as that may seem by today's standards, there was wisdom in this process. Parents knew their children and knew what type of mate would be able to appreciate or even "put up with" their child's personality type. In addition, there were more practical considerations; arranged marriages were treated as serious business transactions. People married within their own class, so there were livelihood issues to take into account as well as dowries and other financial ramifications of the union.

Yet certain aspects of arranged marriages helped to assure compatibility between the betrothed couple. For example, because couples married within their own class, they shared a common value system. Since they had been raised in similar circumstances and in the same geographical area, certain lifestyle, child-rearing, and household duty issues were well understood and taken for granted. Most people within a certain class shared the same system of faith and beliefs, so what religion to practice and to raise children by was not much of an issue.

A couple could get married and feel reasonably assured that even if the mate was a stranger, once they got to know each other, life would proceed for them as it had proceeded for their parents and earlier generations. A feeling of safety and continuity was built into the entire matter.

How things have changed! Most parents have relegated the task of mate selection to their children without so much as a word to them about what to look for in a mate, how to go about finding a mate, and what to do when they find one. The socialization process involved in that modern free-for-all called "dating" fails to adequately prepare our young people to make an intelligent and thoughtful selection of a spouse.

Even if we were not adequately trained in the spouse selection process, we need to make sure that our children are sufficiently prepared to date and consider what to look for in a lifelong mate.

- In what kind of family situation was the person raised?
- Does this person value education and vocational training?
- Is this person completing an education and ready to pursue additional training if the job market changes?
- Are the children in this person's family treated with respect?
- Do the parents honor and show respect to each other?
- Has this person been raised to value Christian family life?

These are the types of questions our children must be prepared to ask and seek answers to as they work their way through the premarital social and psychological mazes.

More importantly, we must make sure that our children are armed with enough Christian training that they can do battle against the negative moral data thrown at them by the culture, the media, and even their own dates!

This is not the time to neglect training our children to select an appropriate mate. The staggeringly high divorce rate in our country — even within clergy families — is evidence enough that we have not done our job in raising up our children to accept the responsibilities inherent in making a marriage work. This crisis must not be taken lightly and viewed simply as the result of lifestyle options in a modern age.

We can take preventive action to guard our children against making the same mistakes that too many in our society have made and often make over and over again. We can also take action to aid married couples who are still together but whose marriages are in trouble. This chapter will examine what can be done to help struggling marriages. The church must take the lead in offering resources to stop the trend of marital destruction and initiate a trend of marital healing.

Think about It

Write in the space below ways in which:

- your church has developed ministries and programs to help repair and offer hope to troubled marriages
- your church supports couples in their attempts to seek Christ-centered solutions to their marital problems
- your church has observed what places the most strain on marriages in the church and community and has tailored its ministries to help alleviate those difficulties

Considering the specific needs of marriages in your church and the surrounding community, list below any new programs and ministries that your church could implement that would offer help to troubled marriages.

Focus

The current divorce crisis in the United States has hit the African American family unit as hard as the overall population. Solutions to the divorce rate must address the social problems that affect African American marriages in disproportionately high numbers, such as suicide, homicide, and unemployment. No remedies for the current crisis will make a difference in the long run unless we look to the future of the institution of marriage and address a basic underlying deficiency in our culture: we are not teaching our young people how to maintain and sustain a marriage.

Once the practice of arranged marriages was discarded from our society, we failed to fill the gap with any meaningful marriage preparation rituals or teaching that would offer guidance to our young people as they are maturing, dating, developing relationships, and deciding what they want to do with their lives and how they want to contribute to society as a whole. Two premarital sessions with the pastor a month before the wedding will not help. By then the stage has already been set, the selection has been made, and, if anything, the pastor can only offer quick words of advice for any last-minute questions the couple may have.

As was discussed in chapter 6, the key is compatibility; we must introduce our young people to the concept of compatibility early in their development. And understanding compatibility begins with understanding who God created us to be — a body and a soul.

In Genesis 2:7 we read that God formed man of the dust and then breathed life into him. The human being then became a living soul. In this very short verse we have the essence of human life: the physical — formed from dust — and the spiritual — the breath of life entering the body, which forms a living soul.

This physical/spiritual being can be described as having a head, a heart, hands, and feet. We can look at these four areas as defining who and what each person is. And it is to these four areas someone considering another as a potential mate must look to determine levels of compatibility.

- The *head* refers to the intellect, which encompasses education and training.
- The *heart* refers to our spiritual and emotional being.

- The *hands* refer to the pursuit of common goals.
- The *feet* refer to social compatibility and value systems.

These four aspects must be successfully merged in any successful marriage. Where these components were taken for granted in the closed world of arranged marriages, they must be carefully considered and worked out in the arena where men and women make their own selections. Where common education, religious training, social and value systems, and goals in life were assumed to be the norm when parents made the arrangements for their children's betrothal, two people considering marriage today must determine for themselves how their backgrounds and lifestyles mesh and whether they can establish a lasting level of compatibility.

Once the decision has been made and the marriage is intact, the church can nurture that couple, as described in chapter 6, and provide support for them as they try to maintain whatever level of compatibility they have established for themselves.

But what about the marriage that is in serious trouble? What about the marriage that is at the point of divorce? The "Guideposts" section below lists ways in which the church can step in to offer help and guidance to couples in the midst of such frightening struggles.

The Word

Both the Old and New Testaments are clear regarding God's teaching on marriage and divorce. Genesis 2:24 tells us that the man and woman "will become one flesh" (NIV). That, in essence, is a description of marriage. The two people become one person. Compatibilities merge, values merge, goals are united. The couple shares one vision for the future even if they have different gifts to bring to the attainment of that vision.

In Matthew 19:6 Jesus drives the point home even further. He not only quotes the Old Testament in reminding the Pharisees that the two "shall become one flesh." He then puts the final seal on the matter by adding, "Therefore what God has joined together, let man not separate"

(NIV). *Let no one tear apart.* Let no one try to break up. Let no one divorce. In light of that mandate, what should the church do about divorce?

The church must remain compassionate in all instances. If Jesus did not cast a stone at the woman accused of adultery, the church must not cast a stone at those members who are divorced. The church does, however, have an affirmative mission to see that it does all it can do to *prevent* divorce from happening. In fact, prevention is the key work of the church as it concerns divorce.

When a couple — or as unfortunately sometimes happens, only one of the spouses — has done all that they feel they can do to save the marriage, they need a church willing to say, "Come together under the shelter of the church. Let's see what else we can try." When a couple is feeling uncomfortable with the direction the relationship is going, they need a church that is able to say, "We have something here that should be able to help you put your marriage back on track before things go too far in the wrong direction." The church has a mission to show a better way, a duty to provide a positive alternative to divorce.

Guideposts

Divorce prevention is a churchwide effort to promote the healing of broken and suffering marriages. A church that is sensitive to the needs of married couples in the congregation must rely on the skills, talents, and prayers of not just the pastor, but also of the elders, deacons, Sunday school teachers, and other active church members. When someone senses, sees, or hears something from a couple that would indicate an actual or potential problem in the marriage, he or she must take action to see that the couple receives, or is guided toward, help. Such open concern should not be viewed as malicious meddling or food for gossip. Instead, when done with caring and compassion, it should be viewed as an extension of Christ's love for the church and his belief in the institution of marriage.

In addition to being sensitive to the hurting couples within the congregation, the church must have in place ministries that are actively working to offer guidance and counsel to the church as a whole and that are available to married couples in need of healing. These ministries should include as a basic structure prayer, counseling, and shelter.

Seeking the wisdom and counsel of God through prayer in the midst of marital discord is the first and primary step toward healing and reconciliation. Yet encouraging a couple in the throes of such a marital breakdown to join together in prayer or even facilitating a prayer session led by the pastor may not be an easy task. Often the pain of betrayal or a breach of trust in a marriage is so overwhelming that it can make hearing the voice and counsel of God almost impossible. The breakdown may have reached such a painful stage that the husband and wife can not join hands in prayer — they do not even want to touch each other. Such a crisis point in the relationship can make hearing God's voice almost impossible. At that point intercessory prayer becomes a necessity. The pastor must take the lead in inviting the couple to remain in the same room together while he enters into prayer and seeks the Lord's healing word for them.

Once the healing process has begun, the prayer sessions can become a means for the couple to talk to one another through God. They can pray aloud about the relationship, their visions of healing, and areas where they feel they have been abused or misunderstood. This is a spiritual open forum with the pastor serving as mediator in which the couple's relationship can be nurtured to the point where they are ready and willing to hear — and act upon — God's counsel. Whatever level of prayer ministry a couple needs, the important point is that prayer must be a vital part of the services offered and readily available to couples at all stages of marital healing and growth.

The second essential component to an effective marriage healing ministry is a counseling center. This center will take two forms. First, it is equipped to handle one-to-one sessions between the couple (or the spouse willing to receive counseling) and the counselor. Next, it produces and promotes churchwide seminars and workshops on subjects that adversely affect marriages and families.

In the first instance the center will be the location for personal marriage counseling sessions with a certified counselor/therapist. A working example of this is the Crisis Counseling Center at Greater Christ Baptist

Church (Detroit). The center is staffed by two licensed social workers and a registered nurse. All three are volunteers from within the church body. The center maintains a twenty-four-hour prayer line. After listening to a brief prayer, callers leave their name, telephone number, and the nature of their call. The messages are retrieved on a frequent basis, and the caller can be contacted within a short timespan. Individual counseling sessions are scheduled once the initial contact is made. The focus of the ministry is to respond to the crisis calls of members of the congregation and the surrounding community. Such a center is also viable as a specific resource for marriages in crisis. Even if the couple requests pastoral counseling in particular, the center is there to respond to other crisis components of the marriage/family situation.

Churchwide seminars and workshops should be a direct result of feeling the "pulse" of the congregation and knowing what personal and social problems are causing conflicts and stress in homes and marriages. There may be a need for substance abuse programs, gambling addiction workshops, or seminars on combating workaholism. All of these social ills have a direct and immediate bearing on the health of marriage relationships in the church. In addition to promoting the general well-being of the church membership and surrounding community, such programs have a direct and positive impact on couples in the church. Even those who are not seeking the personal counseling services of the counseling center will be helped by the outreach of these seminars and programs.

The third essential part of this ministry is shelter. The terms *shelter, safe house*, and *protection* all involve two aspects. First is the general concept that a church should be a place where couples with troubled marriages can go for a "time-out." That is, whether couples are seeking personal counseling, attending a series of church/community workshops, or just enjoying the fellowship of other believers, the church is a place where they can leave behind the worries of the marriage and enjoy a rest from their usual concerns. They will not have the same tendencies to respond to each other as they would in the home surroundings. Nor will they be surrounded by reminders of their troubles — a pile of bills, a disruptive teenager, a cabinet full of medicine — that can prevent even the most well-meaning couple from forgetting their cares for a few moments.

At the church they can take a breather and refresh themselves. When they return home, they hopefully will view their situation with a dose of renewed hope and expectation.

The second concept of shelter is that of an actual place where a physically or mentally abused spouse can go to escape a dangerous or potentially dangerous situation. Serving the same purpose as shelters sponsored by social agencies for abused women, these would be available either in the church or in the homes of specially designated and trained church members. They would be places maintained for church members who, for safety concerns, must leave the home situation until appropriate measures have been taken to assure their safe return. The location would be kept from general knowledge and would change from time to time to keep abusive spouses from readily seeking out the abused mate. A call to the church would let the pastor or elder direct an abused spouse to the area of the church or member's home where temporary shelter could be obtained.

Needless to say, a church with these prayer, counseling, and shelter ministries in place can play a vital role in the health, well-being, and safety of its members' marriages. It can also play a vital role in the community by being a place where marriages are rescued and revived and not left to the usual recourse of divorce.

Q & A

Question: If a church follows these prescriptions and initiates all of these new ministries, won't most of the church's resources be spent on marriages?

Answer: Yes, and it will be money well spent! The marriage, and hence the family, is not only the backbone of society, it is the backbone of our future. There should be no hesitation to provide whatever funds are available and then seek out some more to assure that our marriages are sound and thriving. Society as a whole benefits when a marriage is functioning as it should. Children are not distracted at school; employees can focus on their jobs; and energy spent dealing with constant marriage problems can be channeled elsewhere. There should be no hesitation to spend as much of a church's available resources as necessary on ministries that aid marriages.

Question: For these workshops, where can I find professionals who are willing to address the social crisis issues from a Christian perspective?

Answer: First, look within your own congregation. It is important to maintain a database, either on computer or on index cards, of the skills, training, education, and certification your members possess. You may have access to all of the resources you need right under your own roof! And these church members would already be in a position to know many of the concerns and crises affecting the membership.

Also, many times, even if a professional does not counsel from a Christian perspective, the prescriptions for health and change are universally applicable. Interview the professional before agreeing to a presentation. Make sure he or she knows what type of program you want for your congregation. If the presenter cannot comply, perhaps he or she can provide a referral to a professional appropriate for your church.

Highlights

Listed below are many of the key components necessary to building a ministry that offers marital healing and support. Add other points essential to establishing your own church's ministry to marriages and married couples.

- We must teach our young people how to maintain and sustain a marriage.
- The church must take preventive action to save marriages that are still together but are experiencing trouble.
- The key to a thriving marriage is maintaining the biblically prescribed concept of compatibility.
- The church has an affirmative mission to do all that it can to prevent divorce.

- Promoting the healing of broken and suffering marriages is an active ministry involving the entire church.
- The church should offer marriage ministries based on prayer, counseling, and shelter.
-
-
-
-
-

Think about It – Again

Given the concepts and prescriptions that have been offered in this chapter, think again about what ministries should be implemented or enhanced by your church to serve troubled and struggling marriages in your church and community.

____

____

____

____

____

____

____

____

____

____

CHAPTER NINE

Single-Parent Households

Up Front

When husbands and wives divorce, when unmarried women have children, when married women have children and become widowed, when married women have children and are divorced or are deserted by their husbands, or when wives die or desert their husbands, the end result is the same: single-parent households.

Single-parent households are nothing new. Even the Bible provides examples. To name just a few, we have the widow and her son who lived in Sidon to whom the Lord sent Elijah; Hagar and her son, Ishmael; Pharaoh's daughter who adopted the baby Moses; and the widow of Nain whose son Jesus resurrected.

These cases are not unique, and single-parent households appear in various forms throughout history. Yet no matter what the financial or social situation may be, the need for emotional and practical support is very similar. Young children without a father need a father figure. Single mothers need child care in order to go to school for specialized vocational training. Others who have been suddenly widowed or deserted are in need of emotional support as they struggle to adjust to their new single status.

Whatever the circumstances, single parents have needs, and the church has been blessed with the means and the resources to step in and make a difference. In a church full of elders and deacons, no child should be without a father figure. In a church that takes multiple offerings each week, no family should be without enough food on the table.

In a church with a working missions board, no single-parent household in the local community — the biggest mission field of all — should feel untouched by the ministries of the church.

Why, then, are so many single-parent households in distress? Why are more single-parent households living below the poverty level? Why are more children from single-parent households being held in juvenile detention facilities?

The answers are not clear and the solutions are not easy. Perhaps the modern church has been slow to recognize the role it has to play in this dilemma, which in recent times has reached crisis proportions. The earliest African American congregations and denominations eagerly embraced their social responsibilities to those in the community with known needs. In the early 1900s African American churches sponsored credit unions, schools, missionary societies with local outreach programs, and businesses in their neighborhoods. The church saw dire needs and responded swiftly and responsibly. But as the various branches of government began to accept more of a responsibility for the social welfare of its citizens, our churches backed off. Instead of letting the government supplement the programs already in place in the community, the black church seemed to let the government programs fulfill the entire need. The church let itself be relegated to a position of saving souls and nothing else.

Certainly, assuring the eternal salvation of as many people as possible is the primary calling of the church. That mission can never be slighted without serious detriment to all of humanity. However, the church has a duty to tend to the temporal as well as the spiritual needs of the people it serves. The two cannot be disconnected without experiencing the tragic social and societal consequences our communities are facing today.

Let the church step up and reclaim its place as provider and comforter to those in need. And let those who are experiencing the greatest need today — single-parent households — be the first to be blessed with the generosity of a church that fulfills the mission of the kingdom of God here on earth.

Think about It

List below ways in which:

- your church has developed ministries and programs to aid and nurture single-parent households
- your church supports single parents in their attempts to raise their children
- your church has observed what the greatest needs are among the single parents in its congregation and community and tailored its ministries to help ease those difficulties

Considering the specific needs of the single-parent households in your church and the surrounding community, list below any new programs and ministries that your church could set in motion that would offer help to these families.

Focus

The African American family has always been deeply rooted in the traditions of the extended family. During the generations when our ancestors were enslaved—and as fathers, mothers, and children were sold to other plantations—those family members and friends who remained were left to fill the gap of the loved one who had been separated from them. If a father was sold away, an uncle or even an unrelated male stepped in as a father figure. The same occurred when a mother was separated from her family: someone else provided the love, nurturing, care, and discipline that the birth mother would have provided. Children may have been forced into single-parent situations, but such a situation was never allowed to hinder the child's growth and development.

Even today all of us know of grandparents, an aunt, or an uncle acting as legal guardian to children who have been orphaned by death, incarceration, desertion, or physical or mental incapacity. The tradition of the extended family is alive and well within the African American population.

The crisis exists, however, in the demands being placed on the extended family unit. If statistics are to believed, more than twice as many African American families than white families are headed by single parents. This dramatic increase in the number of single-parent households means that even more unrelated or loosely related volunteers than ever will be called upon to step in to fill the void left by missing parents.

Stepping in does not necessarily mean adoption or obtaining legal guardianship. Rather, it means "being there" when the actual parent's absence would be felt most in the child's life. A male neighbor may play catch with a young boy in the afternoons and discuss his day at school. A college student may visit a family of older children and offer help and guidance with homework. A grandmother may invite some of the children on her block who have two working parents into her home after school so that she can provide nutritious snacks and start them on their homework.

The list of possibilities and needs is so basic that *everyone can do something*. No organized effort needs to be in place for volunteers to contribute time and energy. However, for those who want to be a part of an extended family unit but either cannot fit themselves into a need situation or do not feel comfortable initiating such a relationship on their own, the church can provide an invaluable service to its members by having certain crucial ministries already in place. The church can easily provide the means to connect those who need help with those who can best provide that help.

The church is in a strategic position to be aware of and respond proactively to the needs of the congregation and the surrounding community. Elders, deacons, the mission ministry, Sunday school teachers, children's church organizers, even ushers and greeters must be charged with the task of listening, watching, noting, and referring to the pastor or other designated persons situations that require immediate attention. There is no time to lose. The church must not neglect to do what it is charged to do — reflect the headship of Christ. There are many examples of what the church can do to fulfill its mission to its members and to the community. Later in this chapter we will see how some of these ministries work and the difference they are making to single-parent households that make use of these services.

The Word

The responsibility we have to care for single-parent households — individually and through the church — is clearly defined in both the Old and New Testaments. The modern phrase "single-parent household" is referred to in its most basic form in the Bible: "widows and orphans." In biblical times the patriarchal society treated these two classes of people as nonpersons. They had no rights without a male "redeemer" who could bring them back into their rights within the family structure. A primary and compelling example of this situation is that of the widow Naomi and her young, also widowed, daughter-in-law Ruth. It took the heroic and persistent action of their "kinsman redeemer," Boaz, to bring them back into their family's line of inheritance.

The Bible acknowledges the helpless situations of these two classes of people in Isaiah 1:17, where we are admonished to "defend the cause of the fatherless [and] plead the case of the widow" (NIV). Notice the legal terms used — "defend" and "plead." It is an acknowledgment that widows and orphans have no rights. They are helpless and ignored, in a position to be abused and taken advantage of. As they were over two thousand years ago, so they are now.

Who is their advocate today? Who will stand up for them? Who will see that the widow — the single parent — and her young children receive adequate health care or will cut through the red tape to see that they receive the benefits that are due them? Working on behalf of those who have been denied a voice for centuries, it will take a strong sense of advocacy to recognize that a veritable revolution in thinking and behavior is needed on the part of our society to lift single-parent households from the level of second-class citizenship to the level of full rights and recognition. The Bible is calling us to start such a revolution.

In addition, in James 1:27 we are encouraged to "visit the fatherless and widows in their affliction." It does not get plainer than that. Visit. Take action. Make the first move. See firsthand their housing conditions and the types of neighborhoods in which they live. And, then, once you have visited and seen for yourself, *do something for them.*

A compassionate heart can see that an orphan needs a father figure, but it takes a person willing to live out that compassion to actually volunteer to become a mentor to that child. A compassionate person can look at a teenage mother with her child and tell that she does not have the resources or training to properly care for the infant. But it takes a person willing to live out that compassion to spend time with the young mother and teach her to properly bathe, nourish, dress, and otherwise care for the child.

God does not require that we do anything extraordinary to comply with the mandates of his Word, but he does require that we take a stand and act affirmatively on behalf of those whose voices are neither recognized nor adequately heard.

Guideposts

Programs that meet the needs of single-parent households do not require renovated facilities or elaborate promotion. They do, however, require dedication and a desire to make a difference in the lives of children and single parents.

Three programs that have successfully enriched the lives of countless youngsters and single parents in the congregation and surrounding community of Greater Christ Baptist Church (Detroit) are male mentoring, female mentoring, and the Stork Club.

We will consider, in detail, how these programs work and what is required to start and maintain them. In addition, we will consider a planned Adopt-a-Senior program that ministers both to elderly adults and the families with whom they have been paired.

The Greater Christ Baptist Church (GCBC) male mentoring program grew out of a concern for the intellectual, emotional, and spiritual development of young males in the church and surrounding community who were growing up without the consistent presence and guidance of a father figure. The program allows youngsters in elementary school to come in contact with African American males of various professions and trades on a weekly basis in order to bolster their aspiration levels and self-esteem. In addition to the weekly scheduled activities, the mentors introduce the youngsters to various educational and cultural activities that are suitable for their particular age and stage of development.

The mentors are primarily recruited from the GCBC congregation, although some men from outside the congregation have volunteered to participate as mentors as a result of the excellent reports of the program that have circulated throughout the community.

The youngsters join the group in one of several ways. First, a mother or a grandmother from a single-parent home may request that her son be allowed to join the group. Second, someone from the church with knowledge of a particular home situation may recommend that a child without a father figure be assigned a mentor. Or the youngsters themselves may request to become a part of the mentoring program after seeing the other students perform at a Sunday church service or at the Benjamin E. Mays Male Academy.

Once the child is enrolled, he is immersed into the activities of the weekly meetings. These meetings include discussions led by mentors on topics such as self-esteem, decision making, and goal setting. Also during the meetings, the youngsters memorize Bible verses while the adult males lead discussions on how these verses apply to their lives. The boys and their assigned mentors also listen to presentations by visiting speakers on topics such as combating drug abuse and violence in the community. Other weekly meeting activities might include taking part in role-playing exercises on conflict resolution or preparing a skit that describes how to use Scripture to combat evil influences in their lives. Every one to two months the boys and their mentors enjoy a group field trip to a local museum or recreation spot.

Each May, the boys prepare for an ending ceremony that is conducted at the church during a regular Sunday morning service. They receive special recognition certificates and T-shirts from their mentors. During that same time period, the boys take part in a private "rites of passage" ceremony that is separate from the public church program.

The activities of this private ceremony last from three to four hours and are restricted to the boys and their mentors. In this way, the mentors can develop a rites of passage agenda that is unique to the lessons that have been presented to the boys over the past several months, and the youngsters, in turn, can demonstrate to their mentors how well they have understood and internalized the teachings of that year. The following describes *some* of the components of one such ceremony that can be a starting point for those mentoring groups that have never conducted a rites of passage program and are interested in beginning that tradition for their youngsters

The boys enter the meeting room as they would any other weekly mentoring meeting. However, those who are experiencing the rites of passage ceremony for the first time are taken aside and given a pep talk. The mentors explain to them that throughout the evening they will be applying what they were supposed to have learned during the past year. Also, they are assured that there will be no physical violence or harm done to them in any way and that anytime they want to leave the ceremony they are free to do so. Since the ceremony changes from year to year, it is explained to the first-timers that not even the experienced students know what to expect and therefore all of them will begin the evening on an even footing.

The group is then called together, and the youngsters are instructed to form a circle and hold hands. Each one is blindfolded. The blindfolds are used to foster dependence on one another, helping them to understand that no one of them is better than the other. They are then told to lock arms and instructed not to let go of each other no matter what happens. At that point, the mentors begin to walk around the circle and try to break the arm holds. It is up to the boys to help each other maintain their interlocked arms. After this activity is concluded, it is explained to the boys that in this same way, although satan may try to snatch a

Christian away from his faith, it is the responsibility of other Christians to hold on and help that person stay united with the faith community.

While the boys are still blindfolded, they are split into groups of two and taken to different rooms in the building. The temperature in the room is warmer than usual in order to make it harder for the boys to concentrate. Then, they are asked to recite various Scriptures that they should have memorized during the year and to explain what the verses mean to them. If they are not able to remember the Scripture passages, they can not advance to the next level of the ceremony and they are left behind. At this stage, it is explained to the boys that throughout their lives, when they do not learn the lessons that they are supposed to have learned, they will often be left behind.

At various points during the ceremony, the boys are given the option of giving up or finishing the ceremony. No one is forced to finish, and no one is made to feel ashamed if he chooses not to complete the evening's activities. At another point before the end of the ceremony, the blindfolds are removed. It is explained to the boys that this symbolizes their eyes being spiritually opened. However, now that they can see again, they are reminded to rely on what they have been taught and not so much on how things may appear to their eyes.

At the end of the ceremony, two things occur. First, the boys who have remained to the end are asked to look around and see who is missing from the group. The mentors ask the boys to think back on the evening and try to remember when certain boys left the ceremony and why they chose to leave. Then the boys who did not complete the rites of passage are brought back into the room for a form of debriefing and asked why they did not finish the program. After some discussion by these two groups of boys, the ceremony is completed when one of the mentors invites those who have not committed their lives to Christ to do so. Those who want to make the commitment at that time are taken to another part of the building to discuss the meaning of that commitment; they will join the rest of the group later. The other youngsters are led to another room where they relax and share a time of food and fellowship!

The bonding that takes place between the boys and the mentors can never replace an actual relationship with a biological or adopted father, but it can give the youngsters a chance to develop a connection with someone who cares about them and their future. These young men, when they come of age, will have an example to follow and will be in a position to give back to other fatherless youngsters the same care and attention that were given to them.

The GCBC female mentoring program — named Transformation — has similar goals for the young women who are enrolled in the program. However, the age range is higher — grades nine through twelve. Also, most of the young women come from homes where a female parent is already present. The purpose of these mentoring sessions is to augment the teaching that the girls receive at home. In other words, in a female-headed household, the mother may have neither the time nor the resources to teach her daughter about topics such as:

- healthy lifestyles
- etiquette
- basic Christian beliefs
- women's health issues
- appreciation of women's accomplishments (especially African and African American women)
- achieving academic success
- career choices
- developing a life philosophy
- developing leadership abilities
- time management and study skills

These topics are discussed at mentoring sessions, providing a venue for the girls to explore other aspects of their development as young women.

The sessions are held one Saturday per month for three hours. Adult women from the church and community provide leadership as mentors. At the end of the year, a "rites of passage" ceremony is held that encompasses the range of lessons that the young women should have mastered during their weekly sessions. The teens leave the program equipped to become role models for the next group of high school girls.

Although the Stork Club is designed to assist all new mothers, the program grew out of a demonstrated need within the congregation to especially help young, single mothers adapt to the new demands of motherhood. Based on the adage that "it takes a village to raise a child," the young mother is offered support from the larger church family. Each newborn is presented with a GCBC Credit Union account to assist the mother in saving for the child's education. Also, each expectant mother is given a baby shower by the church. Parenting classes are offered with special emphasis on the needs of young, single mothers.

The purpose of the Stork Club is to build more self-assured mothers, especially as they enter the realm of the single, female-headed household. The club is also a means for the entire congregation to show, in a concrete way, the help and support that will continue to be available to the mother — she will not have to raise the child alone.

The Adopt-a-Senior program is another variation on the extended family theme. Joining together members of two and three generations, the program is particularly useful to single-parent households. Meeting together on a daily, weekly, or monthly basis, the schedule is flexible and determined by the needs of the family and the logistical and health considerations of the senior.

Providing a second adult presence within the household, the senior also provides an important "other adult voice" to support the authority of the single parent. In addition, the senior can often offer observations based on wisdom and experience. In return, the family provides the senior with companionship and a reconnection with the needs of society from which the senior may have been prematurely and unnecessarily cut off.

All of these programs and ministries provide a strong, visible network of support and care that the single parent could not find elsewhere under one roof. The entire church can join gifts, talents, time, and resources to assure that whatever may be lacking in the single-parent household is replaced and replenished through the ministries of the church.

Q & A

Question: I like the idea of the male mentoring program, but why do you start at such an early age? Isn't elementary school too young?

Answer: Definitely not! This is the age when boys are most impressionable and most receptive to input regarding their roles as responsible men in our society. Studies have shown that it is during these early school years that negative seeds are sown regarding academic success and the importance of school. Reading and math scores of most African American males drop significantly by the time they reach the fourth grade. There is not a moment to lose. We cannot begin too early to offer positive intervention programs and role models of success and responsibility to these boys!

Question: How do you maintain the connection between the young, single mother who was helped by the Stork Club and the church once the baby passes the infant stage?

Answer: The other ministries of the church must be in place and ready to step in. The male and female mentoring programs, Adopt-a-Senior programs, and others like them must be active to assure that the continuum of care is maintained between the church and the single parent. These ministries — and others — should provide enough of the backup support the parent needs to feel connected to the church and part of the larger "village" family.

Highlights

Below are many of the key points to remember in building ministries that offer physical, emotional, and spiritual support to single-parent households. Include other points that are essential to establishing your church's ministries to single-parent households.

- The church has a duty to meet the temporal as well as the spiritual needs of the church and community.
- Single-parent households have numerous needs.
- The African American family has always been deeply rooted in the traditions of the extended family.
- The duties of the church toward single-parent households is clearly defined in both the Old and New Testaments.
- Male mentoring programs allow boys to meet African American males of various professions and trades in order to bolster the boys' aspiration levels and self-esteem.

- The female mentoring program seeks to augment the teaching young women receive at home.
- The Stork Club is one way the church can demonstrate that it is part of the larger "extended family."
- The Adopt-a-Senior ministry joins members of two and three generations for the benefit of them all.
-
-
-
-
-

Think about It – Again

Considering the ministry and outreach examples that have been presented and discussed in this chapter, think again about what programs your church could initiate or augment to serve single-parent households in your church and community.

____

____

____

____

____

____

____

____

____

____